the Earth Waited

Debbie —
I pray this
book will bless your
heart —
Your — sister in Christ
Melanie

the Earth Waited

A Christmas Treasury

Melanie Herald Clifford

Expert Publishing, Inc.
Andover, Minnesota

Edited by Pat Morris.

ISBN 1-931945-29-2

Library of Congress Catalog Number: 2004115744

Printed in South Korea

First Printing: November 2004

07 06 05 04   6 5 4 3 2 1

Expert Publishing, Inc.
14314 Thrush Street NW
Andover, MN 55304-3330
1-877-755-4966
www.expertpublishinginc.com

Table
of
Contents

To The Great Giver Of Gifts

I'm grateful, Father, for your gift from above.
Sent down to me from your heart of love.

So in humble thanks, I now give it back to you.
Please use this book however you choose.

Thanks

I would like to thank you Bev, dear friend, for all your support. Without it, I'm not certain this book would have gotten off the ground. Your encouraging words kept me going.

Special thanks go to my prayer group. Audie, Donna, Georgia, Marilyn and Deanna, thank you for your prayers and support.

Thanks also go to my family, who have listened to every piece I have written over and over.

Thank you, Pat, for all your help.

Thank you, Mom, for everything; this one is for you.

The Earth Waited

The Earth waited.

The star shone.

The cattle lowed.

Joseph helped.

Mary groaned.

The baby cried.

The heavens rejoiced.

The angels sang.

The shepherds knelt.

Bethlehem slept.

The wise men searched.

Herod planned.

Jehovah smiled.

A Humble Sketch

God has always had a plan.

In the beginning:
Adam,
Eve

Then came sin:
Satan,
Apple

A fresh start:
Noah,
Flood

A new era:
The chosen,
Patriarchs

The Law:
Moses,
Instruction

Men wanted:
Judges,
Kings

God's prophets:
Ignored,
Killed

Then silence:
Men sinned,
Were lost

God's plan fulfilled:
The Nativity,
Emmanuel

Jesus' Ministry:
Teaching,
Miracles

Christ's sacrifice:
Crucifixion,
Atonement

Man's salvation:
Believe,
Receive

Times ahead:
Second coming,
Judgment

Eternity spent:
Heaven,
Hell

In The Fullness Of Time

God's eternal plan was ready.
The prophets had spoken.
The world's needs were great.
The stage had been set.
His mercy poured out
On a starlit night.
In a stable dark,
In the town of David,
He sent His own Son.
Emanuel, God with us,
A Savior for the world.
God's reconciliation had begun,
In the fullness of time.

Isaiah Prophesied Jesus' Birth

The prophet Isaiah came to Israel to speak,
But most of his words were in vain.
If they didn't repent their future was bleak.
God will not abide idolatry, rebellion, and blame.

From speaking on subjects of doom and gloom,
His message takes on a positive note.
Isaiah speaks about the one on whom
God will send—Christ is our only hope.

Isaiah's message came seven hundred years before,
The birth of our Savior so dear.
Jesus would be born in Bethlehem poor,
Come to wipe away every tear.

Jesus will teach and be a shepherd to men,
But, He'll come again with a mighty sword.
Then He will rule in perfect peace,
And all men will call Him Lord.

Jesse's Seed

Jesse's seed
Everyone is in need;
He has come to intercede.
We will either parish or heed,
Forever grateful for His sacrificial deed.

Oh, Bethlehem

Oh, Bethlehem, through you God would grant
The birth of one with a new covenant.

You are a place many were born and bred,
Looking anxiously for the event ahead.

David anointed and called you home,
But the mighty king was not alone.

Ruth came from you and lived with grace.
You were also Rachael's sacred burying place.

Here God has revealed Himself to man.
You were an instrument in His wonderful plan.

But the greatest guest to you was born.
Our Lord of Lords came that Christmas morn.

"House of bread," how fitting your name.
Jesus, "our bread of life," I'm so glad you came.

Zechariah

Gabriel appeared to Zechariah,
As he served in the temple holy.
Zechariah was a righteous man,
But became frightened and wanted to flee.

The angel said, "Fear not,
For your prayers have been heard.
Thy wife Elisabeth shall bear a son."
Zechariah didn't believe a word.

For both Zechariah and Elisabeth
Were aged in their years.
They had both prayed so long,
And had shed so many tears.

Gabriel explained he had been sent
To tell Zechariah the news.
Their son would prepare the way
For the Savior of the Jews.

"But because of your disbelief,
You shall be unable to speak
Until the child is born."
Zechariah's future looked bleak.

A miracle—Elisabeth conceived a child.
Her barren years were over.
She and Zechariah were overjoyed.
Soon the baby began to stir.

Now it was time for Elisabeth.
She delivered a beautiful son,
Dedicated to God; everyone rejoiced,
For this child would point to the *one*.

Zechariah agreed with Elisabeth,
John would be the name of the infant.
Immediately Zechariah's voice was back.
He spoke of God's plans in that instant.

Now he could talk with the best,
But instead a song he sang.
Singing of the promises to Abraham,
A plan for God's people it rang.

So don't hesitate to pray the impossible.
God is good, and He still answers prayer.
His word is for all to see.
His promises are for all to share.

What Gabriel Said To Mary

God sent Gabriel to the earth to say,
"Mary, you will be used in a special way.
The Lord is with you, do not be afraid."
"I am the Lord's servant," replied the maid.

"God has chosen you to bear His son.
'Jesus,' you will call Him—the holy one.
You are highly favored," Gabriel assured.
"How will this be since I am a virgin?" he heard.

"The Holy Spirit will come. It is true.
The power of the Spirit will overshadow you.
The holy child will be called 'The Son of the Most High.'"
"May it be to me as you say," was Mary's reply.

Elisabeth And Mary

Surprised, they were, by this turn of events,
Elisabeth barren; Mary a virgin.
The news had come heaven sent;
A new chapter for mankind would begin.

Their world would greatly change, for now
The holy God had touched their lives.
This girl and woman with wrinkled brow,
Waiting for their babies to arrive.

Elisabeth said, "God has taken my disgrace."
Then she prepared for John to be born,
Thankful her unhappy years had been replaced.
Childless, she had been forlorn.

Jesus' birth is announced to Mary,
And the news of Elisabeth too.
She learned of the miracles they would both carry,
Then off to the hill country she flew.

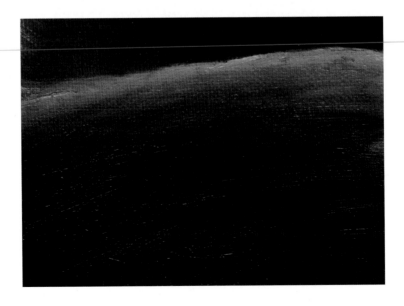

To Judea, Mary went traveling,
To stay with Elisabeth a while.
A greeting to her hosts, while entering,
Mary said with a smile.

At the sound of Mary's voice
Elisabeth's babe leaped in her womb.
She was filled with the Holy Spirit.
Then spoke to Mary, to whom

Was blessed among women.
"And blessed is the fruit of thy womb."
She spoke this all to Mary, and then
Welcomed her into the room.

Elisabeth finished in a song.
A message of encouragement she sang.
It was meant to help Mary along,
Speaking of belief it rang.

Praising God, Mary started to sing.
The *Magnificat* came from her lips,
Thanking God for the privilege He would bring.
Then humbly she began to worship.

Two women, one young and one old,
Through faith, trust, and obedience.
Were part of the greatest story ever told,
A story of God's divine providence.

What Did The Light Reveal?

What did the star reveal that night?
What shone under that awesome light?

The long dusty road from Nazareth.
Joseph and Mary together with

A donkey walking toward the town
Of Bethlehem small and of little renown.

A lonely stable set back from the inn,
Now ready to hold David's kin.

Fields nearby full of sheep,
And tired shepherds fighting sleep.

Angels proclaiming, "A Savior's been born.
He will be lying in a manger worn."

And from the fields a path to lead,
The shepherds to witness this mighty deed.

The brilliant light shown bright and far.
The Magi's direction came from the star.

Just think if you had stood on a hill,
Could you have ever gotten your fill

Of the events taking place that night,
With Christ's own star shining down so bright?

An Essence

Can you picture just a bit,
When the angels came and lit
The heavens with God's glory?

I'm here to confess,
The picture does impress,
But I'm unable to take it all in.

For I have a finite mind,
And this was an infinite sign,
Sent from the Father above.

So I will carry in my heart,
An essence—only a part
Of who God truly is.

Thank you, Father, for the peek.
Now, forever, shall I seek
More of you each day.

Two Separate Worlds

The Messiah, Earth bound and Heaven sent,
Two worlds united for that special event.
Two separate worlds collided that night,
Illuminated by the glory of God's heavenly light.

Shepherds in the fields; Magi coming from the East,
The innkeeper, Herod, and Herod's chief priests,
An obedient couple, and the angels on high,
A stable where the precious baby would lie.

Two parallel worlds—Heaven and Earth,
Brought together for the Savior's birth,
By the power and authority of the Father's hand.
Thus setting into motion His sovereign plan.

The Angels Appearing

And there were in the same country shepherds abiding in the field keeping watch over their flock by night.

And, lo, the angel of the Lord came upon them, and the glory of the Lord shone around them: and they were sore afraid.

And the angel said unto them, "Fear not: for, behold, I bring you good tidings of great joy, which shall be to all people.

For unto you is born this day in the city of David a Savior, which is Christ the Lord.

And this shall be a sign unto you; ye shall find the babe wrapped in swaddling cloths, lying in a manger."

And suddenly there was with the angel a multitude of the heavenly host praising God and saying, Glory to God in the highest and on earth peace, good will toward men.

Luke 2:8-14 (King James Version)

**It must have been wonderful, marvelous, overwhelming,
Awesome, impressive, majestic, and moving.
Can you imagine? Can you place yourself there,
Listening with the shepherds in the cold night air?**

Glory

*And lo, the angel of the Lord came upon them: and the glory of the Lord
shone around them: and they were sore afraid.*
Luke 2:9 (KJV)

The shepherds caught a glimpse—just a glimpse—of:

The incredible brilliance
The awesome radiance
The glorious magnificence
The fearsome beauty
The majestic splendor

Of our Jehovah God

Doesn't it just leave you speechless?

Let Us All Praise The Lord

"Do not be afraid,"
Is what the shepherds heard.
This brought them to attention.
They hung on every word.

"I bring you good news,"
The angel declared to them.
"Great joy to all people,
Today in Bethlehem,"

"Has been born to you,
The Christ, the Savior, the Lord."
Prayers had been answered,
God's love had been outpoured.

"This is a sign,"
The angel's words were ringing.
A baby wrapped in swaddling clothes,
And in a manger lying.

Suddenly, Gabriel was joined
By a multitude of angels,
Praising and singing, "Glory to God,
In the highest," where He dwells.

The shepherds spoke and hurried off,
To see if it were true.
They saw Mary, Joseph, and the baby,
And suddenly they knew.

They went out to spread the word.
All were amazed with one accord.
Then like the angels, the shepherds began,
Glorifying and praising their Lord.

Let everything that has breath praise the Lord.
Psalm 150:6 (New International Version)

Immediate Response

The shepherds heard.

They heard the good news,
The angels sang.
Throughout the heavens,
The good news rang.

The shepherds went.

They decided quickly,
"Let us now go to Bethlehem,"
To see what had been
Made known to them.

The shepherds found.

They found the stable,
Back of the inn,
Mary and Joseph,
And the baby within.

The shepherds told.

They praised and they glorified
Their God that morn.
Then they told all who would hear,
"The Savior has been born."

Just The Beginning Of The Story

To the shepherds the angels sang,
"Peace to men of good will."
A lasting peace of inner soul
Graciously given still.

And then they were gone.
The sky had lost its glory.
But that quiet, empty sky
Was just the beginning of the story.

The Innkeeper

A knock on the door,
"Now who could that be?"
Harried, his wife snaps,
"You go and see!"

The innkeeper goes,
And is ready to scold.
He finds a young man
Waiting out in the cold.

Exasperated, "I have no room.
You've come in vain."
The desperate traveler
Starts to explain.

"My wife's time has come,
What should I do?"
"I'm sure someone else,
Has a place for you."

"They are all full.
I've asked at each door."
But the innkeeper knew
He could take no more.

Outside the innkeeper
Saw the young woman.
By the look on her face,
Her labor had begun.

His heart softened,
"I can offer my stable."
Then under his breath,
"At least it is not full."

The couple was shown
To the stable out back.
It was hard not to stumble,
The night was so black.

The innkeeper asked,
"Will you be all right?
Come lie over here."
He felt for her plight.

Joseph gathered hay
To make her a bed.
And a place for the baby
To lay its sweet head.

Concerned, Joseph watched.
Mary looked so worn.
But now the stage was set
For the Christ to be born.

That Light

The innkeeper was late
At his business that night.

He blew out the lamp,
And was puzzled at the sight.

As he crawled into bed,
The room was still bright.

The last thought he had was,
"What is that light?"

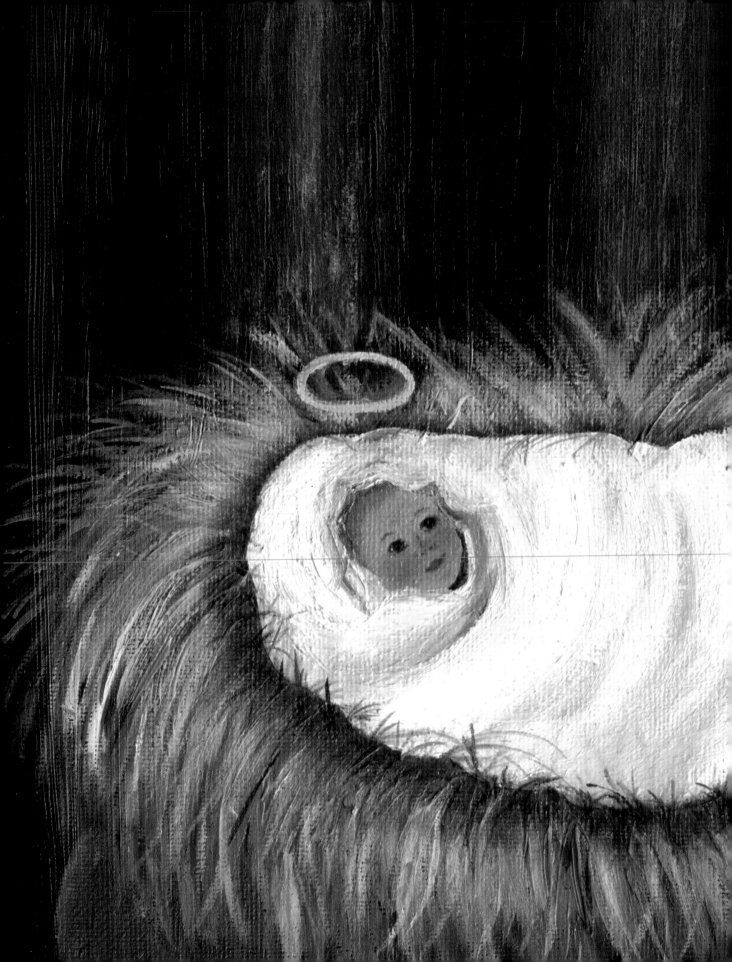

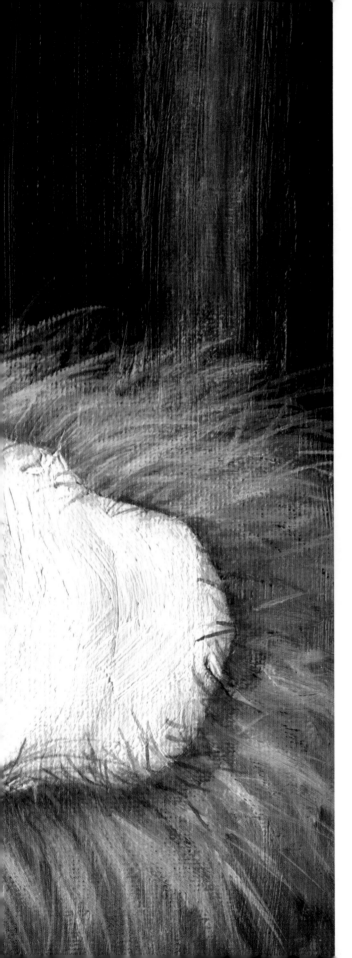

An Innocent Child

An innocent child was born that day.
Come to Earth to show us the way.

Wrapped up in His swaddling clothes,
Moving and wiggling His pink little toes.

Warm and comfortable in His mother's arms,
At least for now out of danger and harm.

Squeaky noises and small little cries,
Looking up into His mother's eyes.

Seeing a blur and a shadow of light,
He would soon have company tonight.

And then the world would begin to know
Of God's son born in the manger low.

An innocent child was born that day.
Come to Earth to show us the way.

How Could Mary Understand

How could Mary understand?
When she held her newborn son,
This baby was the *one*.

How could Mary understand?
When she held His little hand,
The universe He could command.

How could Mary understand?
The baby she took to her breast,
The Romans would arrest.

How could Mary understand?
When she looked at His sweet face,
He was God's plan of grace.

How could Mary understand?
When she soothed His infant cry,
The world would soon know why!

How could Mary understand?
The reason He had come,
This baby who would soon become

Our Savior sent to die.
How could Mary understand?

Joseph, Thou Good And Faithful Servant

A lonely manger made of wood.
Over it, Joseph, the carpenter, stood,
Looking down at the child that was born.
That glorious first Christmas morn.

Amazed, Joseph was by this turn of events.
Tho, for centuries prophets had cried their laments.
The Earth waited for this child so sweet.
The prophecy of old would now be complete.

Gabriel had appeared to Joseph to say.
That the Christ was to come in this special way.
From a lowly maiden full of grace,
To be born in this very unusual place.

A census had brought them to Bethlehem.
God in His wisdom had long had a plan.
This Christ, this Son, Emmanuel,
Was born to take on the sins of all.

The journey from Nazareth had been hard and long.
For days the couple had traveled along.
Mary, weary and heavy with child,
Turned to Joseph, who looked back and smiled.

A stable they had finally found.
As Joseph readied, Mary lie down.
He knew that soon this child would come.
Mary's travail was over. She now had a son.

He loved this child, although not his.
Joseph believed Mary when she explained. "It is
The Son of God, through the Holy Spirit,
To be born to me of such little merit."

The star was bright, the light shone clear.
Joseph was aware that men were near.
Shepherds from the fields the angels drew,
To come and worship this child so new.

So he smiled and tried to understand
This work of Jehovah's he'd witnessed first hand.
Tonight he would watch over and take good care,
Of the child and the mother resting there.

—◦◦—

"Travel to Egypt," the angel warned of death,
Then back to Nazareth after Herod's last breath.
Joseph would watch Jesus grow wise and strong,
Marveling at this child who could do no wrong.

And when it was time for his life to be done.
Joseph was proud of his masterful son.
Surely he must have heard with great extent,
"Well done, thou good and faithful servant."

The Magi

Now when Jesus was born in Bethlehem of Judea, in the days of Herod
the king, behold, there came wise men from the east to Jerusalem.
Matt. 2:1 (KJV)

These Magi were men of astronomy,
Had studied the stars for years.
Joining forces, on camels' backs, they agree,
To start out when the new star appears.

Saying, Where is he that is born King of the Jews? For we have
seen his star in the east, and are come to worship him.
Matt. 2:2 (KJV)

Expecting great celebration in Jerusalem,
Gentiles, they ask for the King.
"Where is this one to be born? We have come.
We have tributes for the child to bring."

Then Herod, when he had privily called the wise men,
inquired of them diligently what time the star appeared.
Matt. 2:7 (KJV)

Coming to the court of Herod the Edomite.
Again, "Where is this King to be born?"
The Sadducees quickly named Bethlehem the site.
Lying, Herod disguises his scorn.

When they had heard the king, they departed; and, lo, the star,
which they saw in the east, went before them, till it came
and stood over where the young child was.

When they saw the star, they rejoiced with exceeding great joy.
Matt. 2:9-10 (KJV)

The wise men were excited to again see the star.
Supernatural and in all of its beauty.
It had been so long, they had traveled so far.
To complete their heaven-sent duty.

*And when they were come into the house, they saw the young child with
Mary his mother, and fell down, and worshipped him; and when they had
opened their treasures, they presented unto him gifts;
gold, and frankincense and Myrrh.
Matt. 2:11 (KJV)*

It was quiet now in Bethlehem town.
They came into the house from the cold.
They worshiped the king and before Him fell down,
Bringing Frankincense, Myrrh, and Gold.

*And being warned of God in a dream that they should not return to Herod,
they departed into their own country another way.
Matt. 2:12 (KJV)*

They found out Herod was not as he seemed.
He would not come to worship the King.
Instead, evil Herod started to scheme.
Death to the firstborn he'd bring.

But God's plans are greater than all!
A warning, to another route they fled.
Hate and jealousy was Herod's downfall.
And it was *his* death recorded instead.

The Gifts Of Wisemen

Gold Speaks Of Jesus' Birth As King

The wise men came to worship Jesus,
Bringing gifts of gold for a King.
Our tribute to Him should be thus,
To give Him our everything.

Frankincense Speaks To Jesus' Life As God

Sweet gum from Boswellia trees
Coming from the desert on camels,
The Son of God, meant to honor thee,
Our praise, a sweet and savory smell.

Myrrh Speaks Of His Death

Myrrh from earliest times has been prized.
Aromatic gum, used for wrapping the dead.
Some thought He was gone. What a surprise!
Oh, sweet joy! He arose instead.

Do You Ever Wonder?

Do you ever wonder?
About those wise men from afar.
How they made it to Bethlehem
By following a shining star.

Do you wonder about Caesar Augustus?
Ordering a census to the man.
Bringing Joseph and Mary to Bethlehem
Had always been God's plan.

Or do you wonder about the shepherds?
Tending sheep on the hill.
Hearing angel's praises from above
Must have surely been a thrill.

Do you wonder how the innkeeper felt?
Almost sending the couple away.
At least with the stable,
Mary and her son now had a place to stay.

Do you wonder how Joseph felt?
Looking at Mary and her son.
Seeing the little child in his mother's arms,
And knowing He was the *one*.

Do you wonder about that tiny babe?
Born that wondrous night.
The shepherds came and kneeled in awe,
At this perfect and beautiful sight.

Do you sometimes think
On all this and wonder if it's true?
Believe it! For like Mary, Joseph, and Jesus, His Son,
God has a plan for *you*.

Prophecy Fullfilled

Jesus the Christ born in Bethlehem,
The perfect root from Jesse's own stem,
Called to save but not to condemn.

In a lowly stable far from home,
With Joseph, the virgin bore the *one* alone,
Who would sit on the right of his Father's throne.

The angels sang, the star did shine,
God's glorious message they came to define.
Shepherds worshiped this baby divine.

Weeping in Ramah and throughout the land,
Children dying by the soldier's hand,
Taking orders from Herod's command.

Out of Egypt they were warned to flee,
Then back up to Nazareth by Galilee,
To live and fulfill God's prophecy.

Truly God's Son

Surprised, Mary found herself,
With child from the Holy Spirit.

Some people, even learned ones,
Profess they don't believe it.

Man's mistrust, fear and unbelief,
Comes straight from the pit.

Remember? Jehovah our God and Creator
Commanded, and the sky was lit.

———◆———

Startled by this troubling news,
Gentle Joseph wouldn't hurt her.

But to this godly Jewish man,
The ancient law was clear.

That they would stone young Mary,
Became his greatest fear.

Joseph decided to divorce her quietly.
His love for her sincere.

———◆———

He was thoughtful and confused.
Things were not as they seemed.

Then the Lord spoke to Joseph,
Through an angel in a dream.

"Take Mary as your wife."
This news was the angel's theme.

Young Mary and Joseph's life,
God the Father would redeem.

———◆———

Mary had her sweet baby boy
In a stable by the inn.

Jesus, He was to be named.
They were instructed therein.

Jesus—Emanuel—God with us.
On a cross He would be pinned.

But, halleluiah, on that third day,
Victoriously, triumphantly, gloriously,
God's son rose again!

Jesus, Son Of God And Son Of Man

He left His glory behind Him.
And came as a tiny babe.
He left his Father to do a job,
Born to the Jews to save.

He existed in Heaven forever.
His family to Nazareth returned.
His work had been to create the world.
Use of carpenter tools, He learned.

He is totally and completely omniscient,
Yet would study in synagogues.
He lived in the heavens with angels.
His rulers wore Roman togs.

He is part of the Godhead Triune,
Owned no place to lay His head.
He had no beginning and has no end,
Yet from David's seed He was bred.

He is forever omnipresent,
Yet walked through the country to teach.
He who knew his Father's great love,
Abandoned by countrymen each.

He is Holy above all others,
Tempted but never sinned.
Angels sing "Holy, Holy, Holy."
Yet to a cross His body was pinned.

He, who willingly gave up His life,
Could command ten thousand angels to save.
But instead in quiet obedience He endured.
To His tormentors, He forgave.

He who came down as a baby,
Now sits on God's right hand.
This was the birthright of our Savior.
Jesus, Son of God and Son of man.

The Bright Morning Star

I, Jesus have sent my angel to give you this testimony for the churches.
I am the Root and the Off-spring of David, and the bright Morning Star.
Rev. 22:16 (NIV)

Born under the radiant Christmas star.
If you could gather light from near and far,
Jesus' light would outshine them all.

Not the light of kilowatts or rays.
Or the sun's heat that brightens our days,
But a heavenly one that changes lives.

His light was from the beginning, you see.
He made the stars for you and for me.
He just spoke, "Let there be light."

He saw that the light was good,
Pleased at the sight from where He stood.
We need light to make our way.

His light will open up your mind,
Into the darkest heart it can shine.
The most profound teachings are made clear.

If your nights and days seem dark,
And all that you do seems too miss the mark,
There is an open invitation to partake.

So get ready for the light of life,
For those with a thirst and sick of strife,
Call on the Son of the bright Morning Star.

And He will find you just where you are,
The blessed Son of the bright Morning Star.

Christ Is Our Peace

Glory to God in the highest and peace on earth good will toward men.
Luke 2:14 (KJV)

PEACE: Not of man's making.
                Look at our sin.

PEACE: "There is none," saith the Lord.
                Look at the world.

PEACE: Made possible by the Savior.
                Look to Jesus.

PEACE: Received by faith in Christ.
                Look to God's gift.

PEACE: To men of goodwill.
                Look to His providence.

PEACE: Deeper than external feelings.
                Look to His Spirit.

PEACE: Of mind and soul.
                Look to His restoration.

PEACE: Lasting, not temporal.
                Look to eternity.

PEACE: Assured at His second coming.
                Look to His promise.

God Incarnate

God incarnate, you came to dwell with us.
The world looked on, asking, "What's all the fuss?"

But I've come to know from reading your word.
What a wonderful sacrifice has occurred.

You left your Godhead, your crown and your throne.
Born in a stable where the star brightly shone.

Instead of angels worshiping at your feet,
You were laid in a manger where cattle eat.

For you left your kingdom and lived with man.
From time immortal this was God's plan.

But still the world asks, "What's all the fuss?"
Answer—Salvation through God's Son who died for us.

"Lord Of Lords" And "King Of Kings"

Jesus, "Lord of Lords,"
Born of the kingly line.
Your people had waited long.
God's decision: it was time.

Throughout Jewish history,
The generations came and went.
Abraham, Isaac, David, and Solomon,
Then the "King of Kings" was sent.

You had the perfect pedigree.
You are the perfect one.
Sent to redeem this sinful world,
The loving Father's Son.

You accomplished your Father's work,
In a manner loving and strong.
But some wanted an earthly king,
Man can be so wrong.

For your kingdom is in heaven.
Well, also in the heart of man.
You sit on the right hand of the Father,
Some day I will stand.

And I will see you face to face.
My soul will be set free.
Then along with the heavenly host,
I'll cry, "Holy, Holy, Holy."

I'll sing to my "Lord of Lords"
And to my "King of Kings,"
Holy, Holy, Holy
Holy, Holy, Holy.

Angels Rejoycing

In the beginning God created the world,
And the angels watched with interest.
He spoke, His powers to employ.
Then the angels shouted for joy!

And then came the time foretold,
The Son of God would be born.
And at the birth of Jesus our King.
Jubilant Hosts began to sing!

Scriptures tell if just one sinner,
One man, comes to God in faith.
And if he repents of sin by choice.
In the heavens the angels rejoice!

And when this same believing man
Arrives at the end of life,
Consumed his time on earth to roam,
Angels joyfully carry him home!

Someday what a sight we'll see,
Myriad of angels encircling the throne.
"Worthy is the Lamb," they sing.
Honor and Glory and Praise they ring!

The Lamb's Book Of Life

Caesar Augustus decreed a census
No one could ignore.
He demanded that all should go
To their birthplace, rich or poor.

The emperor wanted to know
The population, the amount,
To see about the taxes,
To make a good account.

Mary and Joseph traveled home,
So they, too, could enroll.
The government wanted an accurate amount,
So it could take its toll.

Much of the population
Moved about the land.
Each coming home to register,
Written by each hand.

The census book showed the record
Of each and every one.
Each person was accounted for,
When the job was done.

But there is another record book
Of far greater import.
In heaven it resides,
Stamped, our heavenly passport.

I thank you, Lord, for faith.
It's written in your word.
My name is in the Book of Life.
I've already been registered!

I sing honor and glory and praise!

Brand New Bikes

I got a bike.
Mick got a trike.
The colors were alike,
Both red and white.

On Christmas eve night
Under the lights
Shiny and bright,
Folks smile with delight.

Their gift was just right.
Oh, what a sight.
Two little tykes,
So happy tonight.

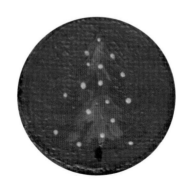

The greatest gift of these is love
1 Corinthians 13:13 (NIV)

Unconditional Love

When I look back on my childhood,
A smile spreads over my face.
My parents were always there for me.
You see, most of my memories are good.

Not that we didn't have trouble.
Illness plagued my young body for years.
But my life was a wonderful respite,
In spite of the fears my Mom would quell.

Thinking about the little house in town,
My folks, brother, and Aunt Elma.
We never thought of riches or power.
Our bower, bathed in love all around.

Oft times when Mick and I asked for a nickel,
Three hands were outstretched with a coin.
Happily, not aware of our blessing,
Guessing would we buy candy or popsicle?

We were neither a prince nor a princess,
For allowances, we needed to work.
Daily making the beds, cleaning the bath,
The path of responsibility to possess.

I never needed to prove myself
To my folks or Elma or Mick.
It makes life easier for a child,
While gaining self-esteem for oneself.

In our world we didn't grow up fast.
We played with all our strength,
Biking, games, and fun at the pool,
Cool waters after the hot sun at last.

We didn't need to do great things.
And were allowed to make mistakes.
It is easier to take on something new
If you don't feel the pressure failure brings.

We all ate together at night as a family,
5:30 around the large table.
Laughter and talk were our main course
To reinforce our family daily.

As I say, my folks didn't have riches and such,
But they gave us their time and attention.
Unconditional love, the best inheritance we give,
To live lives with a loving touch.

I wish everyone had had the love.
I'm saddened by the hurt of others.
We live in a selfish world, I'm afraid.
Man-made rules, but I know of

One thing I have found throughout the years,
Sitting down with someone's story.
I know God's love can ease their pain.
It's plain; Abba will wipe away their tears.

Old Memories

Sometimes old memories creep into my mind,
While decorating my tree I remembered the time

When Dad, Mick, and I went to Erdman's tree lot.
Coming home excited, "Mom, look what we got!"

She smiled and commented on the beauty of the tree.
Then turned and called, "Elma, come out and see."

Dad sawed and wrestled the tree into its stand.
We all stood back and thought it looked grand.

The tree needed to sit for an hour or two.
So we sat down for supper of Mom's beef stew.

We listened to Crosby, Clooney, and Como,
Christmas albums playing on the family stereo.

Mick and I did the dishes while Dad moved the tree.
The living room corner was the best place to see.

Dad helped with the lights—bulbs of all colors.
Mom put the tree skirt around the stand on the floor.

Next came glass ornaments red, gold, and green.
Some were the prettiest that I had ever seen.

But there were other decorations for our tree.
School and Sunday school crafts made by Mick and me.

A box held some old ones from years gone by.
Plastic angels had once caught someone's eye.

We draped many garlands of silver and gold,
And fresh strings of cranberries and popcorn unfold.

To apply silver tinsel, Elma pieced and Mick jumped.
There were hundreds of pieces; I threw it in clumps.

The tree was topped with an angel of white.
That was Dad's job; six-foot-one was his height.

Now my Christmas tree is a thing of great beauty.
White lights and decorations for all to see.

But I remember clearly the ones I once saw.
Simpler things made us stand back in awe.

Caroling At The Nursing Home

I belonged to our small church choir.
We had been practicing our music for weeks.
For our program, our leader required.
Somewhere to practice our technique.

An invitation from the nursing home.
Located two miles out of town.
Inwardly, I started to groan,
But there was no turning around.

Saturday we met at the church.
Everyone seemed to be there.
Waiting on a pew I perch.
We will be leaving soon, it is clear.

I'm not very excited to go.
My attitude is not what it should be.
I walk out of the church very slow.
Happy if I could just flee.

We get in the cars and head out of town,
Laughing and kidding each other.
We get to the home and start to unload
Our group, including my brother.

Walking inside, we go through the halls.
We are starting to create quite a stir.
One old lady sits with a shawl,
To an invisible person, "Thank you, sir."

As I pass, I look into the rooms,
Small spaces in which to live.
An ancient gal is holding a broom.
I wonder whom she has outlived.

We are told to go to the center,
To a room in which all have gathered.
As I pass I notice one old dear,
She looks like a small fragile bird.

A few rooms have some Christmas cheer,
A poinsettia or tinsel around.
I began to think we possibly were,
Doing something quite profound.

We arrived at the center, got ready to sing,
I looked around at the audience.
Most were there, others, nurses would bring.
I hoped this all made sense.

Many were seated, cardigans pulled tight,
Brown leggings falling down around ankles.
Some stared into air, some had no sight,
Complexions white as eggshells.

As the Christmas carols continued,
Something happened to the crowd.
There was a positive change in the mood.
Quite a few were singing out loud.

One old gent came to the front.
He must have loved music indeed.
He led the next song without comment,
Then Mrs. Johnson came back to lead.

Some were feebly moving to the music.
Others rocked gently back and forth.
One tapped his cane—click, click, click.
Another singing for all he was worth.

Three young people sat in wheeled chairs,
For different reasons I assume.
Sometimes life doesn't seem fair.
They will live lives in one small room.

Up came a little gray-haired lady,
Touched my shirt just as a carol had begun.
Afterwards I thought just maybe,
She had one like it when she was young.

I discovered that I was my problem.
I felt an amazing change.
My heart had been overcome.
This had been an equal exchange.

We were bringing Christmas, we thought.
But instead they brought it to us.
This is one lesson we were taught.
Our lives were enriched and thus

We completed our concert with "Silent Night."
Now many had tears in their eyes.
These people had given me insight.
For there, by God's grace, go I.

Christmas Carols

It's Christmas eve; we are all getting ready.
The car is packed with the goodies.
Among them resides my daughter's teddy
And gifts for under the tree.

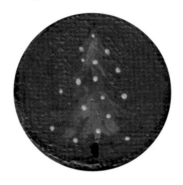

Each Christmas we arrive at Aunt Margaret's.
"What smells so good, Mom?" "It's roast turkey."
Bringing food to share, mine buttery spritz.
Back then nothing was calorie free.

"Hello, Pat. Hello, Sandy," hugs all around.
Comments, the kids are growing so fast.
Everyone must be here by the sound.
Three little boys march past.

Margaret's house is now bursting with family.
We have multiplied over the years.
Grandma, aunts, uncles, cousins. Let's see.
Yes, my whole family is here.

Everyone is excited about Christmas.
From the very young to old, it is clear.
One of the babies is making a fuss.
Grandma's grinning from ear to ear.

Adults seated around the large table.
Others scattered throughout the house.
Some helping those that aren't able.
Young marrieds sitting close to their spouse.

Buttery lutefisk is passed around.
And warm stacks of lefse, too.
Vegetables, salads, potatoes by the pound.
And a big pot of oyster stew.

We eat our meal with loud talk and laughter.
Plates full of our favorite food.
Christmas dinner becomes just a blur.
Full tummies, everything tastes good.

Finally the last plate is empty.
But now coffee and desserts are served.
"Is it time for the presents?" kids yell with glee.
"How about dishes?" Margaret observes.

That it is Christmas, it is easy to tell.
For the men are doing the dishes.
My aunts chime in, "Please do them well,"
Laughing, "Take your time, this is what our wish is."

The children are playing impatiently.
Astonished at how long it takes.
Uncle John puts a child on his knee.
Giving her tired mommy a break.

The last dish is wiped, the towel is hung.
Teasing, "Any dishes we overlooked?"
A hue and a cry come from the young.
"Is it present time?" said with a hopeful look.

"You've forgotten about Christmas music," reminds Nan.
"Elma has the books, send them around.
Melvin, and Mick would you give them a hand?"
They pass out red books paperbound.

Judy sits down at the old upright piano.
She practices while we find a seat.
Soon the melodies start to flow.
The old carols that sound so sweet.

The first song we all try to follow the tune.
Some good voices, some not so good.
Working up to the notes we are soon,
Loud but at least now we're understood.

The second song, "Hey, we're all right."
I look at Rodney, Jim, and Dad,
Parroting barbershop, what a sight.
We laugh and say, "How sad."

"Jingle Bells" gets a mighty, "Hey!"
Pat and I try different parts.
On "A one horse open sleigh.
Hey!," this music could go off the charts.

Susie and Wanda are singing quietly.
Mom and Nan share a book.
We are all working on staying on key.
Catching our breath, the children mistook.

They think this is the end of the songs.
Laughing, we point at the number.
Sorry, but your assumption is wrong,
We're just getting into high gear.

Another one asks, "Will we ever be done?"
Elma answers, "We have more to go:
"Angels From the Realms of Glory," "Oh Come
All Ye Faithful." Beautiful, don't you think so?"

We start, "Oh, Little Town of Bethlehem,"
Singing with all of our might.
This old Christmas carol is such a gem,
Telling of that wonderful night.

A personal favorite, "What child is this?,"
"We Three Kings" brings back memories.
If not sung, we would be remiss.
Let's sing them all, we agree.

Singing carols, hitting the notes with ease,
Sandy asks, "What about 'Silent Night?'"
A four-year-old pipes up "Please."
We answer, "This is the last one, all right?"

Grandma's old, now her voice is weak.
But once "Silent Night" was her solo.
I look around and take a peak.
Grandma's singing, her face all aglow.

We're done; tradition complete for the year.
The children run to the tree,
Together they send up a mighty cheer.
This is what they want, you can see.

It's fun to watch as they open their presents,
Many of them handmade.
As adults we sit and are content.
The music is just starting to fade.

The children are playing with their presents.
We adults try just one more dessert.
I say of the pie, "This is heaven sent."
My boys say their tummies hurt.

"This is good," Grandma said with a smile.
Her speech thick with a Danish accent.
Uncle Carl added, "There is no denial."
We all knew exactly what she meant.

It's getting late, and it's time to go home.
Children need to be in bed.
"Drive carefully," instructs my cousin Jerome.
We put on warm jackets and hats on their heads.

Driving to my parents with our children,
We agree this was a special night.
It's almost too quiet after the din.
"This is good." Grandma was right.

Come Celebrate

Come celebrate the birthday of a King.

Let the church bells ring!
Let the choirs sing!
Let your heart take wing!

Come celebrate this wondrous thing!

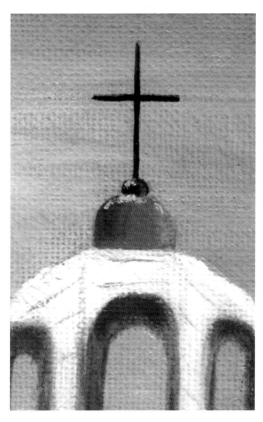

Extra, Extra, Hear All About It!

A special edition—Listen
　　　To God's messengers.

The word is out—Shouted
　　　From the heavens.

Notification announced—Pronounced
　　　From God above.

The good news proclaimed—Aimed
　　　At our sin.

An incredible story—Glory
　　　To God in the highest.

Joy

Joy to the world, the King has come.
Thank you, Father, for sending your Son.

Joy to the world for Christmas eve.
Thank you, Father, for the faith to believe.

Joy to the world for loved ones dear.
Thank you, Father, for your blessings this year.

Joy to the world for all that I see.
Thank you, Father, for your goodness to me.

Joy to the world for your loving kindness.
Thank you, Father, for solace and rest.

Joy to the world for my children and theirs.
Thank you, Father, as believers we're heirs.

Joy to the world for the gift you have given.
For through your son, Father, I've been truly forgiven.

Gifts

Under the Christmas tree.
What a beautiful sight.

Homemade gifts that took many a night.
Frivolous gifts to bring delight.
Heartfelt gifts say, "Hug me tight."
Unique gifts that are dynamite.
Expensive gifts, shiny and bright.
Unplanned gifts not quite right.
Practical gifts will shed the light.
Antique gifts are a birthright.
Surprise gifts meant to excite.
Perfect gifts with great insight.
Family gifts planned to unite.
Precious gifts for this special night.

The greatest gift, Jesus the Nazarite.

The Most Precious Gift

It's Christmas eve, we have gathered together.
Coming from near and far.

The meal was delicious, then a plea.
"Let's open the presents under the tree."

Colorful gifts wrapped and collected.
"That one is pretty," a little girl said.

"Go pick it up," she is told.
"The one wrapped with paper and ribbon of gold."

She toddles over to the Christmas tree.
Bending down lower so she can see.

Picking it up she brings it to Mama.
We watch, interested in this small family drama.

"Open it," our chorus rings aloud.
She looks up and around at the smiling crowd.

She begins to tear the bow away,
As her sister explains, "It's Jesus' birthday."

Out of the box comes Jesus in the manger.
She recognizes Him; He's not a stranger.

Now she's excited; she's done something grand.
She hangs on tightly, with her sweet little hand.

As Grandma says, "Jesus is our most precious gift."
Her Daddy comes close and gives her a lift.

To the crèche where there is an empty space.
Jesus is laid in His special place.

Touching the floor, she jumps for joy.
This Christmas she helped God's baby boy.

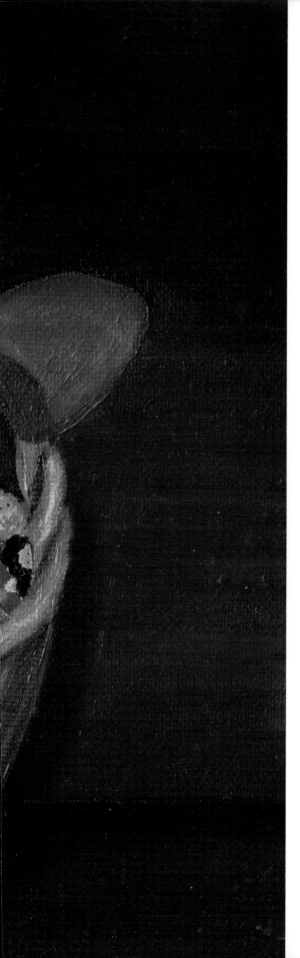

The Toy Store

Traveling with my granddaughters,
We stopped at a Christmas toy store.
Each of the girls was excited
To go in and begin to explore.

"You may each purchase one item," I said.
A price was then preset.
The clerk spoke to me with concern.
"You have only five minutes left!"

A look of great determination.
Came over each little face.
The race was on. Brynne,
Four years old, quickly set the pace.

She picked this up, "Forget it!"
To another she said, "No, sir!"
Hurrying, scurrying, each item dropped.
She soon became a blur.

Now geared up, she was wasting no time.
For there was none to spare.
Examining each and every piece,
We were all beginning to stare.

Swiftly, she ran from place to place.
Steadily gaining speed.
Hoping feverishly that her time
She would not exceed.

Scouring, inspecting, searching,
Concentrating with all of her might.
Quickly assessing, considering.
"Nope!" No toy was quite right.

Like a little red-headed hummingbird,
Brynne flitted from place to place.
But finally she slowed down a bit,
Looking closer at a particular space.

She stopped and picked up something
From a basket she had been spying,
Looking up at me. I walked over
To where tiny babies were lying.

The other two saw her dolly,
And quickly to Brynne they headed.
Decisions made, what a relief!
The siege of the toy store had ended.

Trimming The Tree

Sitting back I decide just to listen,
And watch as the girls trim the tree.
Granddaughters, now there are nine.
All busy as busy can be.

Down from the attic they came,
Each box opened and regarded for beauty.
"Oh, look at this one," Cecilia exclaims,
As they search through the Christmas tree booty.

They start hanging garlands with glee.
"But it's getting all twisty," Brynne giggles.
Shaking my head, "It looks good to me.
"Kori, hold that end." Emma catches the middle.

The lights on, the garlands complete,
Kari tweaked and finished the task.
"Congratulations," I call from my comfy seat.
"Why don't you open that red box?" I ask.

The red box holds all of the angels,
Treasured ones saved from the years.
"Everyone, this one's from me," Emma tells.
Shenae grabs. "She'll break it," Cecilia fears.

Boxes of ornaments bright and shiny,
Each beautiful in primary colors.
Shenae holds one in her hands so tiny.
Baby Jessie watches the others.

"This one is so pretty," Lydia squeals.
Its surface reflects her sweet face.
"Put it on the tree," Cecilia explains, "We'll
Help you reach that high place."

Kari, the oldest, comes to the rescue.
She lifts Lydia way to the top.
Gently Lydia attaches the bulb.
All agree, it's the perfect spot.

The decorating is now down pat.
They work as an organized team,
Even disguised the part that was flat.
Mari, "I just love this angel theme!"

Finished, they admire the tree for its beauty.
Claiming this is the absolute best.
Turning back they looked at me.
I agree, saying, "There is no contest."

"Where is the hot chocolate and cookies?"
They all ask as they rush to my chair.
"You promised us goodies," they tease.
Laughing, I go to prepare.

Brown Christmas

We have a brown Christmas this year.
Most greet this with fairly good cheer.
But others would like it white.

I look out the window at the snow-less expanse.
Peering at the heavens, is there a chance?
But the skies are clear and bright.

"It's not going to snow," I overhear.
Someone adds, "Let's get on with Christmas this year."
I turn and smile and say, "All right."

The men bring the tree in from the cold.
Upright in its stand, the branches unfold.
The piney smell is a delight.

Decorating with garlands, bulbs, and tinsel,
Even our memories, we manage to excel.
When we turn on the lights,

Sitting and talking in front of the fire,
Everyone comes and sits to admire
The flames burning bright.

Mugs of hot chocolate, each with a cookie.
It doesn't get better than this, we agree.
Granddaughter Lydia hugs me tight.

I look out again at the dark night sky.
What is this? Something has caught my eye.
I see clearly the cross on our church tonight.

Weather doesn't matter, I discover again.
Heat, snow, or even warm showers of rain.
Because Jesus was born on a brown hill that night.

Wise Girls

This Christmas we've enlarged
Our grandchildren total by four.
Our son married a gal with three;
Together they had one more.

It hasn't been the easiest thing,
Blending family traditions.
But it is very important,
Especially to my son.

Each year I help my
Granddaughters give a little play.
This year they were "Wise girls"
Performing Christmas Day.

We met in the den,
Robes red, silver, and green.
I helped dress each girl,
Prettiest wise girls you've ever seen.

They all became quite serious,
As we waited in the hall.
I turned on the music,
And hiked up one gold shawl.

I had made each a crown of jewels;
They were dressed and looked so sweet.
Each girl carried a present,
To lay at Jesus' feet.

Each one walked by herself,
To lay the present down.
Parents and guests looked and listened.
A dignity the girls had found.

Every one had her moment,
They all had their chance
To be part of something special.
All sang, the littlest danced.

We felt this a memorable night.
The audience was wowed.
Tonight had been a joint affair;
They all grabbed hands and bowed.

Anticipation

As a child I couldn't wait:
>
> For Christmas to draw near.
> What would appear
> Under the tree this year?

When I was young:
>
> I opened presents with glee,
> A dolly, a teddy,
> And a tea set for me.

Once I got older, the presents changed:
>
> A turquoise princess phone,
> An outfit Mom had sewn, and
> A ring with my birthstone.

It was still exciting:
>
> I received lots of books,
> Clothes by Bobbie Brooks, and
> A hand mirror in which to look.

Still later I received:
>
> From my handsome groom,
> A comfy chair for the living room, and
> My favorite sweet-smelling perfume.

I still enjoy opening gifts:
>
> The granddaughters have a crafting spree.
> These are the best gifts we all agree.
> "Hurry, open it, Grandma, and see!"

So as a Grandma I receive:
>
> Pictures of their sweet faces.
> Drawings of outdoor spaces.
> "Colorfully" painted flower vases.
> Simple embroidered pillowcases.
> Not to mention braided bracelets.
> And, best of all, lots of warm embraces.

Jesus' Pure Light

The new falling snow
coming down so white.
Was it this cold
back on that special night?

Clouds cover the moon,
the stars out of sight.
An involuntary shiver
gives me insight.

Into the dark, cold place
He was born in spite
Of the star from the heavens
burning so bright.

But deeper, I think,
knowing quite right,
My heart was as dark
before Jesus' pure light.

*For all have sinned
and fall short of the glory of God
and are justified freely
by his grace
through the redemption
that came by Christ Jesus.*
Romans 3:23, 24 (NIV)

Consider Me

Consider me, Lord,
And all that I've done.

The sins I've committed,
Yes, Lord, every one.

There's no place to go,
There's no place to run.

He graciously reminded me,
"I've sent you my Son."

What Do You Think?

Some *only* think of Jesus as
That sweet baby in the manger.

Some think of Jesus as
That kind and loving teacher.

Some think of Jesus as
That gentle quiet healer.

Some think of Jesus with
Outstretched arms on the cross.

Some think of Jesus as our Savior
Sent for our redemption.

Some think of Jesus sitting
At the right hand of His Father.

Please set your mind to thinking
And your heart to believing!

More Time With Him

Have you heard?
"Half the fun is in the planning," they say.
Thinking, I place my cup on the tray.
It's true, but there is so much to be done.
Planning a party for God's Son.

Let's see,
Shopping and cleaning should make Him glad.
Baking and decorating—I'm going mad.
Each year gets busier than the last, I fear.
But is this all there is to this time of year?

So I asked,
What would my Savior have me do?
I thought and pondered, finally a breakthrough.
Christ doesn't want *things* that we can give.
He just wants our hearts in which to live.

Yes, a plan!
I'm purposely slowing down this season.
Scratching off items from my list for a reason.
I will spend more time in worship of Him.
Who came to the world to save us from sin.

Thank you, Lord.
So, joyfully I come to worship the King,
My heart ever grateful and ready to sing.
Of wonders and miracles He has done. It's true!
The same He will do for me and for you.

What Shall I Ask For?

What shall I ask for this Christmas?
I really have all that I need.
Giving and receiving, what's all the fuss?
Wanting heaps more could simply be greed.

What have I gotten through the years?
Things interesting, some not, I'll admit.
I've received gifts that have brought me to tears,
But is it worth all the money, I submit?

What on Earth do I really need?
Warmth, clothes, shelter, and food.
Much more is *want* I'm sure you'll concede.
I need a check in my attitude.

What I really want, not that gifts are wrong,
From loved ones is time and attention,
Tenderness, compassion from the heart belong.
Gifts like kindness and respect won't end.

God's word tells, "Love thy neighbor as thyself,"
The most wonderful gift we can give.
This I really want to do, I thought to myself.
Jesus knew this is the way we should live.

I have found, on my own, I find the task hard.
I try, but oftentimes fail.
Excuses aplenty, Satan tries to bombard.
I ask for Christ's help; He tips the scale.

Wanting and needing are two separate things.
I'm sure that we can all agree.
So with my heart in my hand, I go to the King.
Please help me love unselfishly.

What If He Hadn't Come?

What if He had not come that day?
What if God hadn't sent Him our way?

Throughout the years the prophets heard.
God said He would, and He keeps His word.

I don't want to think of my life without Christ.
I am awed and humbled at His sacrifice.

He gave His life, so that we might live.
He shed His blood, so God could forgive.

For many, Christ still has not come.
Please, won't you turn toward the Holy One?

Heavenly Music

As the lights go down, the mood has changed.
The crowd is hushed, musicians arranged.
A baton is raised and without delay,
The renowned orchestra begins to play.

On that quiet night the shepherds slept.
The safety of their sheep they kept.
The light shone bright and they were sore afraid.
God's new covenant the angel made.

As music fills my mind and heart,
I almost feel I am taking part.
At times it quietly drifts along,
Then powerfully the sound becomes so strong.

Shepherds listened to the angel and feared.
Suddenly a multitude of angels appeared.
Singing joyfully of God on high,
A host praising Jehovah from the sky.

The music takes me back in time.
To the heavens my mind starts to climb,
Trying to imagine how the shepherds felt,
Listening to music from where God dwelt.

The celestial chorus sings, "Peace on Earth."
Proclaiming the news of our Savior's birth.
But there is no peace under the sun.
Only in the heart when you accept God's son.

The finale has ended; I'm back with a start.
The music has touched me and opened my heart.
As we slowly walk out into the cold night air,
I look up at the heavens; thankful He's there.

What Does Christmas Mean To Me?

What does Christmas mean to me?
It's not the gifts under the Christmas tree.

Or the house decorated with hundreds of lights.
Even though it's a beautiful sight.

Or the baking of breads and cookies and candies.
I don't even want to start counting calories.

Or the cards I've addressed and the messages written.
This year's theme is angels and children.

Or the gifts that I've bought and carefully wrapped,
Hidden so well, I'll need a map.

Or the menu that has been planned for a month,
Down to the decision on the best Christmas punch.

Or the special dress bought for that holiday party,
Where everyone talks and the laughter is hardy.

All of these things are good, you see,
But the things that mean the most to me

Are Christmas eve services with singing and light
Meant to touch our hearts with delight.

Family and friends gathered to worship the King,
Hearts full of love and lips ready to sing.

The story of angels singing a Christ child has been born.
Follow the star; you can be there by morn.

The looks on my granddaughters' faces when told
Of the love of Jesus who was sent from old.

I'll take time for myself to think on all this.
The miracle of our Messiah I don't want to miss.

So I'll try not to focus on bustle and fuss.
But on the wonderful gift God has given to us.

And when the last ornament has been stored away.
I'll carry in my heart, my Savior born that day.

Christmas Cards

I sit here at the table,
Writing out Christmas cards,
To each a special greeting,
To each my warm regards.

While working down my list,
Sometimes I feel sad.
For many names I've had to cross out,
But then, I also add.

For some this is the only contact
I have with them each year.
But writing them at Christmas
Seems to bring them near.

I suppose this job takes longer
Than it really should.
But memories come and linger,
I'd go faster if I could.

I save my Christmas cards.
Call it my recycling part.
It is hard for me to toss.
Each beautiful work of art.

I send out special cards
That speak of God's salvation.
They tell the wonderful story
Of God's redeeming Son.

This isn't a burden,
It's something I like to do.
For it's good for all of us
To hear the story anew.

I set the fire under the water
For a hot cup of tea.
Now it looks like I will need
At least two or three.

A Lost Art

One of the greatest gifts
I believe anyone can give
Is a listening ear.
And as long as I live

I will appreciate the *time*
That has been granted to me
By those who are kind,
Even sometimes when we disagree.

Conversation is a dialogue,
The sharing of ideas.
Thoughts tossed back and forth,
To think on and respond to because

It loosens up the heart,
And the mind and the spirit, too.
Some things you never knew you knew,
Until the ball gets tossed back to you.

So picture this, if you please,
Good company and a pot of tea.
Sitting across and sharing your life,
A lost art, some would agree.

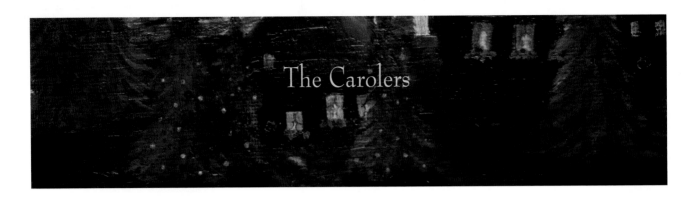

The Carolers

Sitting in my chair, I think
I can hear someone singing.
Then another sound,
Could that be sleigh bells ringing?

I get up from my seat,
And go to explore.
I walk down the hall,
And open up the door.

Surprised, I recognize faces
Standing in the crowd.
I smile at cheerful voices,
Singing out very loud.

"Please do sing another,"
I gently implore.
Asking the crowd of neighbors,
Of a dozen souls or more.

Pairs of shining eyes,
And red rosy cheeks,
Through the sea of legs,
Little Victoria peeks.

Their hats, scarves, and mittens,
Are now dusted with snow.
But clearly the weather,
Hasn't hampered this show.

Christmas song books in hand.
"Is there a request?"
I answer, "'Silent Night';
I've always loved it the best."

"Would you like to come in,
And warm up a bit?"
"Thanks, but we have many places to go,"
They laugh, "We can't afford to sit."

Their songs are now finished,
They prepare to move on.
"Thank you so much," I say.
And then they are gone.

I went back to the family room,
And sat down on my chair.
Laying my head back,
I pray a little prayer.

"Oh, thank you, Lord, for kindness,
And love and, well, for everything.
Thank you for the songs so sweet,
And the blessings that they bring."

Crystalline Art

I put my coat on for a walk in the woods,
Grabbing mittens and scarf from the chair.
Opening the door and there I stood,
Taking in a deep breath of cold crisp air.

The crunch of my boots hitting the ground
Brings back a memory. I think hard.
Then I remember my grandfather's sound,
As his boots hit the snow in his yard.

The woods are quiet and a little dark.
Birds scatter as I pass by.
Soon the trees thin into a park.
I stop and look up at the sky.

Entranced I watched as a little child,
Remembering the importance of snow.
A gray squirrel shakes it off, and I smile,
Both enjoying the glorious show.

Large flakes are drifting down slowly.
What had I done when I was young?
Suddenly I forget about old sensible me.
Opening my mouth, I let one land on my tongue.

We all know snowflakes have no taste.
But the chill left a tingle instead.
I realized snowflakes have a special place.
They are each different, somewhere I had read.

I let one land on my coat sleeve.
And looked closely at the intricate design.
Its pattern I could never start to conceive.
A work of art in frozen crystalline.

In God's world nothing is by chance,
No matter what anyone says.
Look around you, you'll see in a glance.
He is the great artist in all of His ways.

It Just Doesn't Matter

Christ's birth date questioned way back then,
December, January. Is it really important when?
But it just doesn't matter, and this is the key,
For Jesus has come for you and for me.

The wise men came a few months later, it's clear,
To visit Bethlehem, and this child to revere.
But it just doesn't matter, and this is the key,
For Jesus has come for you and for me.

Trees and holly have a pagan beginning,
But innocent use just can't be sinning.
But it just doesn't matter, and this is the key,
For Jesus has come for you and for me.

Santa Claus is a problem for some.
For others Christmas is what he's become.
But it just doesn't matter, and this is the key,
For Jesus has come for you and for me.

Numerous people have made the decree,
Too many of gifts under the Christmas tree.
But it just doesn't matter, and this is the key,
For Jesus has come for you and for me.

We gorge and we drink too much juice from the vine.
Holiday partying has been put on a shrine.
But it just doesn't matter, and this is the key,
For Jesus has come for you and for me.

The commercialization many attempt to dispel,
While malls are busy trying to outsell.
But it just doesn't matter, and this is the key,
For Jesus has come for you and for me.

Schools have taken Christ out of Christmas.
Surely, people, something is greatly amiss.
But it just doesn't matter, and this is the key,
For Jesus has come for you and for me.

The fact is God has sent us His Son
To become a Savior for everyone.
And that should matter very much, you see.
For He is the *WAY* for you and for me.
For Jesus has come for you and for me.

An Early Morning Walk

It snowed last night, four inches deep.
I got up early to walk. I just couldn't sleep.
The moon light on the snow, like diamonds it sparkled,
But none of these jewels could you scoop up and keep.

Pine trees in the park are heavy with snow.
Their thousands of lights paint a spectacular show.
An old band shell is outlined and lit.
The brilliance of the lights makes the grounds all aglow.

I pull my scarf tight on this dark winter's morn.
Shivering, "It's gotten cold after the storm."
I consider the Christmas decorations all around town.
Even better than last year, I could have sworn.

Nearing home, the lights are still on in my neighborhood.
I stopped on my street, and there I stood
Admiring and considering the effort it took
To fashion Christmas fantasies out of lights and wood.

I glance at our roof and see our own star.
Dim in comparison, which brought wise men from afar.
I reflect on the star—its message still the same,
Announcing Christ's birth, this man made quasar.

Two elaborately lit houses, but one in between
Had created a picture much more pristine.
This image that caught my breath and my heart
Was a simple, wooden Nativity scene.

Before I turned and walked to my door.
I looked around at my neighborhood once more.
My eyes stopped at the cross on top of our church.
A beacon of hope you just can't ignore.

Through the window our tree is pretty and bright.
Electric candles on the ledge are casting their light.
Stepping through the door I turn for one last look,
And watch as the morning takes over the night.

The light starts to peek just over the trees.
Darkness loses, as the sun is set free.
The skies start to brighten. My heart, will it burst?
Just for a second, "Is this show just for me?"

The town's thousands of lights dim by and by,
For not one of them can possibly vie
With God's work painted by His own hand,
A new promised day come to testify.

The Christmas Table

The radio is turned on to my favorite station.
Christmas music fills my home.

I ironed the dark green tablecloth this morning,
Then laid it over my old wooden table.

The dishes are placed, given to me by my mother,
An old-fashioned pattern of green and cream.

Glassware comes next, water and stems,
Collected over the years and stored in the china cabinet.

I take out the worn wooden box of silverware,
Another gift, for our wedding—so long ago.

On each green cloth napkin I place a gold ring,
Then set one down by each dinner plate.

A simple centerpiece, a cut crystal bowl.
Filled with sparkling gold balls, nestled in pine boughs.

Glass candlesticks stand on each side of the centerpiece
And six gold candles are placed in the candlestick holders.

The simple brass chandelier hung over the table
Is now festooned with pine garlands, and its lights dimmed.

The decorating, cooking, and baking have been completed.
A Christmas dinner of ham and all of the trimmings is ready.

My husband and I change and wait for our guests.
Both of us have been looking forward to this night.

We can hear their laughter as they approach the door.
The doorbells chime, and my husband walks down the stairs.

He opens the door. "Come in out of the cold," we admonish.
"Take off your coats and stay awhile."

They laugh at the saying. I explain,
"My father always used to say it when people came to visit."

Greetings all around, everyone looks so festive,
Some friends we haven't seen for a long time.

As we start to catch up, we lead them toward the dining room.
"Do come to the table and sit down."

Dick gallantly pulls out a chair for his wife, Lee.
We encourage everyone to get comfortable.

Bev and her husband sit across the table from each other.
Glen admires the decorations. Bev agrees, "They are beautiful."

There is something about a beautifully set table.
Women always seem to like the glow of a dinner party.

I thank my friends and am warmed by their kind words.
Looking around at our guests, "We are so glad you are here."

Dick and Diane are telling their latest funny story.
We all join in on the laughter, and when it subsides

I suggest, "Shall we bow our heads in prayer?"
I take the hands of the two sitting beside me and start.

"Without you, Heavenly Father, these preparations are nothing,
With out you this celebration has no meaning.

On this dark and blustery cold December night,
Your love warms us like this candle flame.

So, dear Lord, we ask with sincere hearts.
Please come to our table and be our special guest."

Laughter and love and goodwill flow from each good friend.
Later I smile across at my husband; this has been a wonderful night.

A Fragrant Offering

The tree is beautiful and smells so good.
For quite a few minutes, before it I stood.
Then I decide to sit down to rest.

I sip my coffee and sit by the fire.
Staring at the blaze I don't seem to tire
Of my own little nest.

I toss pinecones on the flame until they start to flare,
Then their sweet resiny smell fills the air.
It is lovely, I can attest.

Thoughts turn to dear family and friends.
Father, I know on whom I can depend.
I'll go to you on their behest.

I shut my eyes and send up a prayer.
Your presence around me I am greatly aware.
Time spent with you I'll gladly invest.

You seem to fill and permeate my home.
Thanks to you, Father, I'm never alone.
My love for you I will always profess.

Your help, your understanding, your company.
I don't deserve it, but you're there for me.
Why you love me, I'm hard pressed.

Then the thought occurs out of the dark.
Maybe my prayers to you light a spark.
Do my ramblings have some zest?

Does my time, my prayer, when I sing a hymn,
When my heart is full clear to the brim.
Can I hold your interest?

Does my praise rise to your holy presence?
Like the sweet smell of my piney incense,
When I offer you my request.

Then from your word, the Great Jehovah,
Our sacrifice to you is a pleasing aroma.
My prayer to you is on a holy quest.

The Day After Christmas

The rush is over, the Christ child has come.
We've planned and prepared and honored God's Son.

But it is a different feeling after Christmas Day.
As I think of God's gift, my mind starts to stray.

For Christmas eve was all sparkle and fun.
But today it is quiet as I think on the one

God sent to us so long ago,
Sent down from the heavens to so far below.

As I clean up the decorations and put away the mess,
The crèche is last, there lies the baby Jesus.

But Jesus is not a baby anymore, is He?
He's the Christ, the Messiah come to set us free.

So let us not dwell on that baby so sweet.
Instead, the Savior of the world, I'd like you to meet.

Kind, loving, merciful through and through,
Mighty, majestic, to name just a few.

And some day all wrongs will be made right.
He will bring an end to our terrible plight.

I do love that baby so small and sweet.
But I rejoice in my Lord in whom I'm complete.

Thomas Turkey

Let me tell you about Thomas turkey,
A canny old bird indeed.
When Farmer Brown came looking for him,
Tom headed for cover at high speed.

Thomas had devised a warning system.
He trained his hens to squawk.
When he heard the signal, Tom went into hiding.
Each time Farmer Brown went for a walk.

November had passed; Tom should have been safe,
But the situation was still dicey.
Farmer Brown was now stalking him daily,
Turning poor Tom Turkey's heart icy.

Tom had become ever vigilant,
Always looking behind his back.
As soon as he saw Brown heading his way,
He dove under the nearest haystack.

Once while eating a snack,
He saw Brown walk out the barn door.
He looked all around for someplace to hide,
Then hid under the front porch floor.

This was getting ridiculous,
Tom's nerves were shot, you could see.
He expected a lot out of life,
So asked, "Why is this happening to me?"

Thomas watched around the corner,
As the Brown children pulled in a tree.
It was getting close to Christmas eve,
This he could plainly see.

Farmer Brown stepped up his efforts.
But Tom turkey could not be found.
Brown searched the farm through and through,
Even enlisted the help of his hound.

As Christmas eve drew nearer,
Farmer Brown made a grim decision.
He was going to get Thomas oneway or another,
So he loaded his trusty shotgun.

Christmas arrived. He had failed.
Brown stopped looking, for he knew
Turkey was delicious with all of the trimmings.
But so was oyster stew.

So this year Tom ducked the bullet.
But as turkeys go, he was a wreck.
He had worked so hard each and every day.
To keep his head on his neck.

Quiet prevailed, life got back to normal.
Tom came out from his hiding.
The hens looked at him all a thither
He had quite a few on the string.

Thomas quickly forgot all his suffering.
For this bird it wasn't that hard.
Now he was preening and strutting around,
Once again the king of the yard.

The Cherub Choir

"Oh, look, here they come," the cherub choir,
Walking down the aisle for all to admire.
These sweet faces are all we require,
For these little folk can truly inspire.

All jostle into "straight" rows by the alter.
My daughter whispers, "Mom, look over at her."
One little girl waves shyly, a little unsure.
Her family waves back, the pew all astir.

They are eager to sing, each little person.
Scrubbed, dressed in their best, and ready for fun,
Happy and excited to the very last one.
To innocently sing about God's baby Son.

For a moment they are settled, arms at their side.
Parents look on with obvious pride.
But when the music begins order is set aside.
They are supposed to stand still. Well, at least they tried.

"Away in the manger," they shake their heads no.
"No room for a bed," now the song starts to flow.
Cradling, "The little Lord Jesus," faces aglow.
"Lay down His sweet head," they tip their heads low.

One little boy is busy making a face.
Distracted, another pushes him out of his place.
A blond wears a red dress and picks at the lace.
While a freckled face cutie gives her neighbor an embrace.

The first verse they sing out loud and clear.
By the third the teacher's voice you can hear.
Prepared with a Kleenex I wipe away a tear.
Not unexpected, it happens to me each year.

They did a great job, we smile and agree.
The applause was a surprise to them, you could see.
They skipped up the aisle, pleased as could be.
Their love of sweet Jesus, natural and free.

I Am The Daughter Of A King

I am so thankful I could sing.
I found out that I am the daughter of a King.
Isn't this a truly amazing thing?
I am the daughter of a King!

So much for Earthly royalty.
It's hard to grasp the reality,
But it is offered both to you and me.
I am the daughter of a King!

Nothing I've done can make it so.
I'm not worthy in myself, I know.
This great honor to Jesus I owe.
I am the daughter of a King!

Humbly I am aware of my place.
I wouldn't be here without God's grace.
Some day I will thank Him face to face.
I am the daughter of a King!

Focus Changed

I love Christmas and all that it holds,
Especially the salvation story told.

When friends and family come to celebrate,
Like a child I can hardly wait.

I delight in that sweet tiny baby
Who came to set my lost soul free.

But a long time ago my focus changed.
I began to think differently—I'll try and explain.

Christmas was a wondrous event,
But something occurred of greater portent.

My heart quickens at the thought,
Of what the bloodstained cross has bought.

He came as a babe, left as an adult.
Admittedly, His death on the cross was my fault.

For, sadly, my sins put Him there.
Well, mine and yours to be strictly fair.

The stone rolled away, the Messiah rose.
Satan defeated, his case closed.

Thank you, Jesus, for your promises kept.
I'm grateful you willingly paid my debt.

A Winter's Song

The little red cardinal is a hardy bird,
A brilliant spot on my snow covered tree.
I watched and listened and overheard
Him speak to his lady love, then she

Sang back to him from the top of the fence.
I wondered what their song would disclose.
Sunny and crisp, the blue sky intense.
"What a glorious morning, my dear," do you s'pose?

My Prayer

And the angel said unto them, "Fear not; for behold I bring you
good tidings of great joy which shall be to all people."
Luke 2:10 (KJV)

God sent His angels long ago to those far distant fields,
To announce to the shepherds the good news.

Of the Christ child, born that night.
He would be found lying in a manger.

Just follow the star.
And the shepherds did, all the way to Bethlehem.

Here in a lowly stable they found God's only Son. They left and spread the
Word, and all who heard were amazed.

This event happened two thousand years ago.
And we are still amazed.

He has come, this Christ, to give us life.
How thankful I am for this news of my Savior.

Salvation came to the world.
It can't be earned, it is a precious gift freely given.

Jesus has come for all of us.
All who will hear His voice.

My prayer is that this Christmas,
Each one of us will be listening.

Isabelle Lee

These days Isabelle lives all alone,
Three years since the Lord took Harry home.

Lonely, she dreads the holiday season.
With Harry gone there isn't a reason

Some days to even get out of bed.
So many things had been left unsaid.

Trouble aplenty and times have been hard.
Coming in from the mailbox, she looks at the card.

Her sisters are coming to visit, they write.
They will be here early on Christmas night.

"Can't stay long, don't bother for us."
Betty adds, "Although we know how you like to fuss."

"Oh, what can I serve my sisters three?"
She sends up a desperate silent plea.

An idea comes. "I'll need to bake.
I'll serve them tea and my Christmas cake."

Excited, Isabelle now starts to plan.
"I will need nuts and raisins and lots of jam."

Finding her cookbook she turns to the page.
How much will it cost, she is trying to gauge.

Jam, she has plenty she put up last year.
But walnuts and raisins, their cost is quite dear.

Jotting down ingredients, she made up a list.
Adding it up, her hanky gets a twist.

Her sisters come seldom; she wants it just right.
They will all be together again, what a delight.

So how can she pay? She had to take stock.
She decided to sell Harry's funny old clock.

The deed is done, the money's in hand.
She's certain Harry would understand.

Tomorrow up early to start getting ready
For Linda, Jeannette, and their sister Betty.

The skies are gray as she travels to town.
Looking quite pretty, in her blue hand-me-down.

The shop owner, Aikins, beams, "You look so young."
As always, his smile leaves her a little unstrung.

"How can I help you, what would you like?"
Looking around, her blue eyes are bright.

"I need citron and raisins and walnuts, too.
Butter and apples, but only a few."

Weighing the walnuts, she cried, "That's too much.
I can only, I mean, I only need two cups."

Happily, he got her all that she needed.
Adding a bit more to her list, he exceeded.

"Have you a tree yet, Isabelle Lee?
There are a few small ones left, as you can see.

It is late and most people have theirs, I daresay.
No charge if you'll just take one away."

A jovial "Merry Christmas," Aikins exclaimed.
Her meager funds left her a little ashamed.

She put a smile on her face and wished Aikins well.
"I hope you have an absolutely wonderful Noel."

Driving her old truck, over the roads she flew.
Very soon her small farm came into view.

Arriving home, she put her groceries away.
Tomorrow she'll bake. It will be Christmas eve day.

Tonight she will plan, set the table and such.
Using the china her mom loved so much.

The tablecloth and napkins and silverware,
Setting the tea set and cups by her chair.

The tree was ragged and a little bit bare,
But after decorating it, she didn't care.

Peaceful dreams and a good night's sleep,
No restless turnings or counting of sheep.

Looking out her window, it had snowed last night.
Crisp and white, what a beautiful sight.

She put on her old apron that tied in the back.
Then reached for flavorings from the handy spice rack.

Happily, she takes the sugar down from the shelf.
Her mind on the cake, she forgets about herself.

Fragrant cinnamon, vanilla, a little nutmeg.
The recipe is complete down to the very last egg.

Carefully she adds each ingredient to the bowl.
Christmas music from the radio, it's good for her soul.

Peeling, and chopping she readies her cake.
When it's finished, it goes in the oven to bake.

The house smells wonderful, the table all set.
One thing is left, she mustn't forget.

"Please Lord, let this day be a blessing to you,
And to Jeannette, Betty, and for Linda, too."

The knock, the door opened, and there they stood,
Her three sisters, looking so good.

"Come in, do come in, and let me help with your coats.
Betty, I'm so terribly glad that you wrote."

"Something smells good," Jeannette exclaimed.
"I bet it's that Christmas cake, what is its name?"

"Christmas cake," Isabelle started to speak.
The sisters laughed until they were weak.

She seated them down at the dining room table.
"It's good to be here," Linda said with her mouthful.

She served them with love, tenderness, and grace.
Her joy was evident from her radiant face.

The sisters talked, they were jovial and merry.
They laughed and cried when they spoke about Harry.

They were sad to go, it had been too long.
But each one felt that their ties were still strong.

They kissed and hugged and assured of their love.
Betty turned back, smiled, and put on her glove.

Traveling down the road, Isabelle's sisters three,
She watched for as long as she could see.

Back to the kitchen to clean up the mess,
Isabelle donned an apron over her dress.

She sang with the radio an old carol so dear.
The new knock on her door she could barely hear.

But it got louder as she walked to the door.
To her surprise it was Aikins from the general store.

He smiled at her, and it made her heart sing.
Explaining, "There are a few things I wanted to bring."

"Well, do come in, you surely are welcome.
I've baked a Christmas cake. Would you like to have some?"

Canceled Flight

This Christmas, John sat all alone.
Business had taken him far from home.

He called his wife and explained the delay.
"The planes are grounded; I'll have to stay."

"I didn't think you thought so little of me!"
"But, Becky, I can't help it, don't you see?"

It had been a long day; the kids had been bad.
In anger, "I guess they just miss seeing their Dad."

Unhappy, they both hung up the phone.
Hindsight is great; he should have stayed home.

He went to the window and looked out at the street.
The pavement was wet with rain and with sleet.

He thought, "I need to get out of this room.
This place is beginning to feel like a tomb."

He put on his coat and went out of the door,
down in the elevator, to the first floor.

He asked at the desk, "Is there someplace to eat?"
She pointed, "Three doors down; it's a treat."

He pulled up his collar, glad the restaurant was near.
The first shop he passed was a chocolatier.

The candy looked good, he decided he'd stop.
The clerk said he had only minutes to shop.

Then on to the restaurant he walked in a hurry.
Most shops were closing; he started to worry.

The Red Dragon, was open, the sign read, "Come in."
The owner welcomed him with a grin.

"It's so nice to see you on this terrible night."
"Thank you, they have just canceled my flight."

The two started talking. John explained his story.
The old gentlemen sighed and said he was sorry.

He ate his meal, which was good, but not Christmas fare.
Feeling sorry for himself; it just didn't seem fair.

Then the owner came over and asked John if he would
Come with his family to church; it would do him good.

He couldn't remember when he had felt so low.
On the spur of the moment, he decided to go.

The family was happy he'd decided to come.
They all were excited to worship God's Son.

"Please wait right here," said Mr. Lee
As he dug into his pocket and pulled out a key.

The church wasn't far, it didn't take long.
With kind greetings and smiles, he felt he belonged.

His new friends led him to a pew.
People from all walks and races it drew.

The pastor spoke of Christ, God's own Son.
Of angels and shepherds, and when he was done,

The spirit of God flowed throughout the room.
In a second it dispelled every bit of his gloom.

He was thankful for the Christmas review.
He prayed and asked God to touch him anew.

A wondrous thing had happened to him.
And to think he'd decided to come on a whim.

For now, instead of that desperate dark feeling,
His heart felt like it would burst, and he wanted to sing.

Each person got up to greet one another,
Treating him like he was their long lost brother.

They talked and sang all the way home.
The Lees acted like he was one of their own.

He thanked them for their caring and love.
They smiled and pointed to the heavens above.

When he got back to his room, he sat on the bed.
He glanced at the phone, it was blinking red.

John called the front desk and asked of the call.
"It was your wife," she giggled. "She loves you, that's all."

Excited, he quickly dialed his own number.
Now, all his heart wanted was to hear from her.

Her voice was different at the end of the line.
She assured him everything was just fine.

"And I'm sorry that I was so grumpy before.
I just wanted to see you come in the front door."

He smiled and said softly that he understood,
"I'd be coming through that door, if only I could."

He began to tell her of the night he had had.
She stopped him, assuring, "I am so glad."

He told of the restaurant, the food, and Mr. Lee.
"How wonderful, John. God is good, you can see."

Each of his children wanted to speak to their Dad.
The youngest took the phone back, she wanted to add.

"Be speedy, Daddy. Come home. I love you."
"As soon as I can, sweetheart. I love you all, too."

He and his wife talked long into the night.
Outside the world was quietly turning white.

Just before he hung up the phone.
He confessed that he didn't feel so alone.

They finally hung up with their last, "I love you."
He lay down on the bed feeling something new.

A peace had come over him he hadn't felt in years.
He started praying in earnest through his tears.

For God had assured him this very night
That *angels* aren't always out of sight.

Lyle

It was late afternoon, Christmas eve day;
The service was over, a small Christmas play.
All was quiet in the sanctuary room,
Except for the swish of Lyle's heavy broom.

Lyle, the custodian, worked steadily on,
Humming an old favorite Christmas song.
A thorough man through and through,
He carefully swept under each wooden pew.

But as he worked at this menial task,
The question came again, and he asked,
"Why, Lord?" Some memories cut like a knife.
For Lottie, his wife, had been the light of his life.

His mind went back to Christmas' past.
The years had gone by so very fast.
No children, but they had always been happy.
"You're a Lottie fun," he would tease and say.

But Lottie was gone, since way back when.
It had taken years for Lyle's heart to mend.
He'd never spent Christmas alone,
An invitation usually came by phone.

His sister had called him early last fall.
He recalled her message as he walked down the hall.
She wouldn't be having Christmas this year.
Kate invited her to Florida, to spend time with her.

He had told her, "I've had many Christmas eves.
I'll be fine; don't worry about me.
Bess, you go and have fun in the sun.
And, please, give my love to everyone."

The job was finished, it was time to go.
Today the work seemed to go so slow.
Walking past the office, Lyle waved goodbye.
Pastor Dan looked up and caught his eye.

"Goodnight, Lyle, are you feeling all right?
You're looking very tired tonight."
"I'm fine," replied the quiet man.
"Merry Christmas to you, Pastor Dan."

"Shouldn't you be at your sister's today?"
"Well, no… she has gone away."
"Heavens, what will you do tonight?"
"Oh…..I don't know, but I'll be all right."

"Nonsense, come join us; we have lots of food."
"I don't know; I don't want to intrude."
"Emily always cooks more than we can eat,
Come on, we have an empty seat.

"Six o'clock sharp, Emily likes meals on the dot."
Smiling, Lyle quips, "I'll be Johnny-on-the-spot."
He left the church and walked on home.
Thankful that tonight he would not be alone.

Showered and changed, he was ready to leave.
"I can't go empty handed this Christmas eve."
Up on the mantle an object he spied,
Then found a box and put its contents inside.

Before Lyle could knock, Dan opened the door.
He stood on the rug on the foyer floor.
"We're so happy you decided to come.
Emily is serving punch. Would you like some?"

Lyle was quickly ushered to his chair.
The celebration began with Dan's Christmas prayer.
Talk and laughter, the meal was just right.
Lyle enjoyed each and every bite.

The dinner was over, dishes on the shelf.
Emily had protested at the thought of his help.
But Lyle gently smiled and helped with the task.
By working together, the job went fast.

Next thing to celebrate this great advent,
Was to hear of the Savior heaven sent.
To the living room to hear the Christmas story,
All were seated to hear of God's glory.

115

It had been years since he had witnessed this scene.
He watched Dan's children, Jimmy and Kristine.
Warm feelings flowed over Lyle like rain.
Being part of this Christmas had eased his pain.

Song books were brought out and carols sung.
"Away in the manger," delivered by the young.
Soon it was time to look under the tree.
The children opened presents with obvious glee.

Lyle sat quietly watching Dan and his brood.
They had helped him get into the Christmas mood.
The presents were opened, all but one.
One box remained, "Would you hand that to me, son?"

Dan knew Lyle was a man of few words.
So was interested in the request he heard.
Jimmy happily brought the box to Lyle.
Then the old man opened it with a smile.

Out from the box Lyle handled with care,
A wooden crèche he set on the arm of his chair.
"My Father carved this so long ago."
Lyle's wrinkled face was positively aglow.

"From the wood of our old walnut tree."
He passed it around so all could see.
The children sat wide-eyed, not making a peep.
As he slowly extracted the shepherds and sheep.

116

"You see, one day came along a big tornado.
Pa quickly said, 'We'll all have to go.'
We ran and made it safe to the cellar.
Then sat listening in the dark to that big old thing 'beller.'

"The door boards shook, nearly scared us to death."
Lyle paused for a moment to catch his breath.
The children asked, "What happened then?"
"It became very quiet, and that was when

"We started up the stairs. What a mistake.
We heard a big crash. 'For heavens sake,'
Ma said, and prayed for our lives.
Pa yelled, 'Back to the cellar!' We dived,

"Ma, my sisters, and me back on the floor.
Pa started up the steps to the door.
Something was heavy. Something had fallen.
But Pa had the strength of two or three men.

"He opened the door then started out,
'Don't you dare go!' Ma began to shout.
'It's all over, Mary,' he said, then he sang.
'His eye is on the sparrow,' through the quiet it rang.

"We all started up at his command.
Frightened, each of us looked at the land.
The tree had fallen on top of the barn.
The animals were scattered all around the farm."

Lyle reached in the box, breaking the spell.
Three wise men and camels. He continued to tell,
"Yup, my Pa used every bit of that tree.
He carved a nativity for my sisters and me.

"Pa worked on these until they were just right.
And then gave them to us on Christmas eve night."
Next he brought out Mary and Joseph.
Peeking in the box, there was one piece left.

The last piece Lyle handled with reverence.
Someone special, the whole family sensed.
The Christ child lay in the palm of his hand.
This love for Jesus they could all understand.

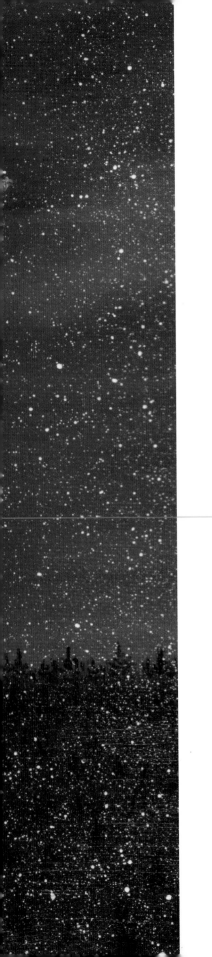

"I asked Pa 'Why' as we cleaned up that mess.
'Lyle, there will always be storms,' he expressed.
'But Jesus will walk through the bad times with you.
Son, I've always found this to be true.'

"Pa was right; he taught us a good lesson.
For my precious Lord has always been the one.
Who has been with me through my tough times."
Lyle was interrupted by the ten o'clock chime.

Lyle smiled as he looked at the children.
And encouraged them to inspect each piece, then
They crowded around his chair,
Happy with him that he was willing to share.

Lyle handed over the box, as he got up very slow.
"I want you to have it, Dan. Now it's time to go.
Yes, please take it," eyes glistened with tears.
Lyle wanted them to have it. He made it quite clear.

"Thank you, Lyle. We will treasure it, but must you go?
Can I take you home?" for it was beginning to snow.
For a moment they watched from where they stood.
"I'll see you in church; the walk will do me good."

Dan watched as Lyle walked down the street.
Then shut the door to the welcome heat.
"It's getting late, everyone to bed.
Christmas services tomorrow," Emily said.

The next morning there was such a crowd.
The choir sang, almost bursting aloud.
But something odd—a box. Interest piqued.
Pastor Dan slowly walked to the pulpit to speak.

Dan swallowed hard, "I'm sorry to say,
Lyle Anderson has passed away."
The congregation let out a sound of concern.
For Lyle's quiet ways, respect and honor he'd earned.

"He died in his sleep, but he's gone to the Lord.
He loved Jesus and that's God's just reward."
As Dan opened the box he said, "I know we're all sorry."
He pulled out the crèche, "Now let me tell you a story."

An Uphill Race
Or
The Tortoise Wins The Prize

BANG! BANG! BANG! The sound of metal hitting metal soon got all of our attention.

It was ten o'clock sharp on a bright crisp October morning, and I was surrounded by strangers ready to make the "run of my life."

It all started with an invitation in the mail. It told of an antique sale near Lake Elmo, Minnesota. *Just another antique sale,* I thought, but I wanted to take my parents on an outing and do a little Christmas shopping at the same time. It turned out to be an outing none of us would forget.

As we walked up the road toward the growing group of people, I saw they were standing behind two men each holding the end of a rope. We joined them and stood waiting for 10:00 A.M.

Looking up the winding driveway, I saw a building surrounded by furniture. Chatting with others, I learned the building was also full, and that this was quite an important antique sale. Dealers had come from around the area to be a part of this annual event.

My folks and I were discussing the fact that it would be quite a climb up the hill. "Well, we will take it easy," Mom said. Both Dad and I agreed. About that time a woman came up to us and asked me, "Are these your folks?"

Surprised by the question I answered, "Yes, they are."

Looking serious she said, "Have you been here before?"

"No," I replied, "Why?"

"When the rope is dropped, everyone will be running up the hill. I suggest you ask your parents to step to the side before hand so they don't get run over."

"Run over?"

"Well," she said smiling, "Just to be careful."

My parents who overheard most of the conversation, looked at each other and wondered what they had gotten themselves into. They quickly agreed. I couldn't run either because of a leg injury. Maybe this trip would be for nothing, and I wouldn't have a chance to purchase the cupboard I was searching for.

As we waited, a few of us buyers discussed what we were looking for. One was searching for a chest of drawers, another a desk. One woman said she had been looking for chairs for her dining room table for months. We were all hopeful. It certainly looked like there was plenty of inventory. Adding to the conversation I said, "I'm looking for a cupboard for my music equipment."

One of the men holding the rope came a little closer to where I was standing and said, "I think I have just what you're looking for."

"Great, what does it look like?"

He described the piece, and we both agreed it probably would fit the bill.

"Where will I find it?" I asked eagerly.

"When you get to the building, go in the front door and quickly turn to the right. My wife will be there, you can't miss it, it will be to your left."

"What do you mean 'quickly'?" I asked.

"You'll soon see, but once you get there, you will need to get a red tag from my wife. If you want the cupboard, sign the tag and slap it on the top, then you will be certain it's yours."

"But what if I want to think about it for a moment?"

"That's about all you'll have," he answered, laughing.

Excited about this news, I walked over to Mom and Dad and told them what the man had said. As I was telling the folks this information, I heard grumbling from the crowd.

Looking at Dad I said, "What on earth?" and then asked the woman next to me, "What's the trouble?"

She pointed to a ravine to our left, an area where there was no restraining rope blocking the entrance. A number of people standing there could be seen edging up the hill, closer to the sale. A group behind the restraining ropes yelled a few comments toward them, but they were ignored. These people were definitely hard core, and the situation was getting very interesting.

I looked at the group of trespassers and could have sworn that each and every one had on a brand new pair of running shoes. Was it my imagination that they were sneering at us law-abiding citizens?

One man standing behind me said in disgust, "Some people don't have any pride; look at them over there, just like a pack of wolves, ready for the kill."

I thought that was a little drastic and asked the gentleman, "Aren't we all here for the hunt?"

"Ya," he said looking at the rope. "But at least we're legal!"

This was getting serious.

Before I could think any more about the rights and wrongs involved, I could sense something about to happen. The entire crowd became quiet. The excitement was electric. I bent down to retie my shoelaces, then asked Mom to hold my purse. I didn't want anything to encumber me.

Every eye was on the front door of the building. Promptly at 10:00 A.M., a woman came out the door—a spoon and a metal wash pan in hand. She started banging for all she was good for, and the ropes fell to the ground.

The crowd rushed through the gate. The race was on. All around me people, young and old, male and female, thin and not-so-thin, were running up the hill. Long strides, short steps, some helping others. All in perfect silence. It was surreal.

I power-walked up the hill, faster than I had ever walked. Most of the crowd sprinted past me. I began to think that I would never get there in time. "Get the lead out girl," I told myself, and pushed on. Finally reaching the front door, I took a deep breath. His instructions were to go in the front door and then take an immediate right. That should bring me to the cupboard, which would be to my left. He had given me his name, so as I approached the area I spotted his sign. Just to be sure, I asked the woman in the booth. I looked to my left and there it was, the most beautiful antique cupboard, a perfect cabinet to hold my music equipment.

About six feet long, it was an old pine piece, honey colored, with a large personality. Yes, I said "personality." I found out later it was hand made years ago, originally for a kitchen. It had shelves for my receiver, tape player, etc, and ten drawers, a perfect place to store my tapes, CDs and DVDs.

I asked for the red tag, signed my name and slapped it on the top. Yes—it was mine!

I quickly walked around the rest of the building, but by then almost everything had sprouted red tags. I didn't see anything more beautiful than my cupboard. My parents found me; they thought it was nice.

"Nice?" I said passionately. "It's beautiful!"

Now to get it home. By then the fellow had arrived minus the rope, and we talked logistics. I paid him and gave him directions to my home. He would deliver it the next day.

When it arrived, it was indeed a perfect match for the space. My husband took a long look at it and shook his head. He has not yet become enlightened to the beauty of old furniture.

My house has many beautiful pieces of furniture, but every time I look at my pine cupboard I smile, knowing how I earned this particular piece, having paid with every ounce of stamina I had. The tortoise won the race of her life.

An Afternoon With Elma
And An
Evening In Paris

"Melanie."

I was so warm and comfortable, but there was that sound again. I rolled over.

"Melanie, come down for breakfast."

Slowly I pushed the quilts away. "Coming, Mom."

Then I remembered it was Saturday, that was a different story. I popped out of bed and ran downstairs. After Mickey and I finished our Rice Krispies, we hurried back upstairs. Shoving our flannel pajamas into the drawer, we quickly made our beds and got dressed.

"Remember, you have practice for the Christmas program," reminded Mom as we walked back into the kitchen.

How could we forget? It had been the main focus in our church since Thanksgiving. Now there were only two practices left.

But today my mind was on other things. After practice, my Aunt Elma and I were going to go Christmas shopping. My Aunt Elma, Mom's sister, lived with us. She took care of my younger brother Mickey and me and helped with the cooking and household chores. Today, Elma was going to help me find the perfect Christmas gifts for Mom and Dad.

As soon as we got back from church rehearsal, Mom and Elma fixed our favorite lunch, of Campbell's tomato soup with crackers.

Mickey and I were both so hungry, we made short work of the soup. Mickey slurped noisily, just to bug me.

We brought our bowls to the counter where Mom was washing dishes. We both picked up a dish towel and helped.

I looked down at my towel, "Hey, I got 'Wednesday's child' and it's Saturday!" I exclaimed.

Mickey and I giggled for a long time at that great joke. All of our towels were embroidered, with most of the work done by Elma, but Grandma Kristofferson and I had also added a few pieces to the collection. Fancywork was an important pastime among the women of our family. At last the dishes were done and now we could go.

Anxious, I called, "Let's go, Elma."

But Mom had other plans. "Let's take a few minutes and decorate the table," she said.

So into the dressers she went bringing out colorful tablecloths, scarves, and runners. All of the linens were made from bright red cotton, with white poinsettias embroidered by Elma. Mom and Elma were a team, working happily together decorating the kitchen. The kitchen was soon transformed. We all stood back and admired their work.

"It really looks nice, Mom, but can we go now?" I asked.

It had been spitting snow all morning, but now it was beginning to snow in earnest.

Our winter coats were in Mom and Dad's bedroom. One entire wall of the room consisted of closets. Our house was a very old one, one of the first built in the town. Mr. Kasson's, like most older homes, lacked storage space. This wall of shallow cupboards and closets held a grand assortment of items, from books and sewing material to Christmas decorations. Our coats were hung on hangers from the door pulls.

Elma and I got our coats, hats, and mittens. I admired my new boots, as I pulled them on, white rubber with matching white fur at the top. I pulled them easily over my shoes. Mom made sure I was snapped, zippered, and tied. Elma slipped her pink wool coat over her shoulders and buttoned the enormous buttons. With a tug she tied her white wool scarf under her chin.

Mickey and I both got allowances—twenty-five cents a week—for doing chores. Actually, lucky us, we got two allowances as Elma always gave us money, too. Last summer we had taken a trip up North and, at a trading post located in the Paul Bunyan park, I bought a small leather coin purse. The Indians made them from deer hide, and it was very soft to the touch. Now mine bulged with coins.

I tucked it carefully into my jacket pocket. Back in the kitchen, I peeled my mittens off the stove and put them on. They were warm and smelled a little of burnt wool—one of the seasonal smells of winter.

"Well, I guess we're off," came from Elma.

At last, I thought to myself.

We had to walk through the front porch to reach the outside door. Automatically, my head turned to the many containers of Christmas cookies and breads piled on the table. Mickey and I had made many trips foraging. The porch, which wasn't winterized, was used as a great big refrigerator.

My eyes rested for a few moments on one special container. It held my favorite Christmas chocolate fudge. Mom and Elma made it every year. I always made sure I was on hand to volunteer my help. Mickey always seemed to appear also. Mom let us help by adding the chocolate chips and the nuts to the marshmallow cream and Hershey bars. She or Elma would then add the hot ingredients to melt the whole concoction, always with an admonition to be careful as we stirred.

Outside, everything was covered with a new dusting of snow. Smiling down at me, Elma offered her hand and I took it. We walked hand-in-hand for a short distance. As we approached downtown, I quietly slipped my hand out of hers. I looked up at her, but she didn't seem to notice. She knew that I was a big girl, already nine years old.

"Oh, look, Elma!" I gasped. "Isn't it beautiful?"

We had reached Main Street, and all the Christmas lights had been turned on. The lights shone brightly against the snow on this dark gray afternoon. Each light pole had its own special decoration with garlands stretched across the street to its counterpart. The greenery and the candy canes were disappearing under the fresh snow.

Of all the stores, I thought the Variety store had the nicest decorations; Elma agreed. Strings of lights framed the many toys displayed in their windows. I stood for some time looking at the games, puzzles, and stuffed animals. At one end of the window I could see a doctor's kit, a holster holding a silver cap gun, and several Indian bow and arrow sets. I excitedly pointed out the dolls. I loved dolls. My current favorites were the triplets I had gotten for my last birthday.

Elma and I walked into the Variety store. The jingle bells tied to the door announced our arrival.

Mrs. Jensen, one of my favorite ladies in town, worked as a clerk. She and I had always had a special friendship. In the spring I would bring her bouquets of lilacs, violets, and lily of the valley from our yard.

With a big smile she asked, "Hello, how can I help you two?"

"I'm looking for presents for Mom and Dad."

Mrs. Jensen asked, "Do you have anything in mind?"

"Yes, but I want to look some more."

"We'll just look around, thank you," said Elma quietly.

We browsed up and down the aisles. I knew the toy aisle well after examining it many times for Mickey and me.

We soon reached the candy aisle. Knowing that Elma liked candy as much as I did, it didn't take much to convince her that we needed some.

"Should we buy our candy here or at Erdman's grocery?" Elma whispered.

I thought about it carefully, "Erdman's has more kinds," I whispered back.

Elma stopped at a display of handkerchiefs and was choosing some for Grandma. The sign above

them read "Sunday Handkerchiefs." My Grandma Kristofferson always carried a handkerchief tucked up her sleeve. Elma picked out three very pretty ones, all pastels—light blue, pink, and yellow.

Mrs. Jensen's brown eyes twinkled. She looked down at me from the counter, "Just a candy bar Melanie? You didn't find anything you liked for your folks?"

"Na," I admitted, and gave her my nickel, "I'm still looking, thank you."

"Well, good luck."

The bell sounded again as we stepped outside. Large flakes of snow hit our faces softly like feathers. We watched as they came floating down from the sky slowly and quietly. We were both delighted. It was a perfect Christmas shopping atmosphere. One of the towns most distinguished men walked by, his beard and mustache white with snow.

"Elma!" I said softly, she leaned down. "He looks like a snowman, doesn't he?" I giggled.

She looked back at the man and started laughing, nodding her head in agreement.

Our small town seemed full of people today. Like us, many were doing their Christmas shopping. As people went in and out of stores, Christmas music was carried out into the street. Elma and I started quietly to hum Christmas carols.

Main Street consisted of three blocks of stores. By now the snow was falling so heavily it was difficult to see the clothing store, Leutholds and Parkins, down the block. I looked up at Elma. Snow was covering her coat and head scarf and even her eyelashes and eyebrows. We were both also beginning to resemble snowmen.

After waiting for a car that was slowly creeping down the street, we crossed over to the jewelry store. The brilliantly lit display window made the jewelry sparkle. We daydreamed for a few moments, then walked on.

We continued on our way, but we needed to walk carefully as the sidewalks were becoming deep with snow. Crossing the street again, our next stop was the Kasson Drug Store, my prime destination.

I went immediately to the case that held the perfume bottles. I had a fascination with one of the fragrances. The blue bottle was extra pretty, its shape cylindrical. Different then the rest.

I took Elma's hand, dragging her to the counter, "What do you think?"

I could see that Elma was as intrigued as I was over this wonderful perfume bottle. She looked with great interest as I explained to her how nice the deep blue color was.

I looked up with excitement, "And Elma, look at the little tassel at the end of the cap, isn't it just beautiful?"

"They are all beautiful, Hon. Is this what you want to buy your Mom?"

"Do you think she will like it?"

"Yes, I'm sure she will," Elma said positively.

The clerk came and asked, "Hi, back again? How can I help you today?"

Pointing inside the case, "Can I see that one again?"

She brought it out and put it into my open hand. The cobalt blue glass was so smooth. I looked closer and read the price out loud. It was marked $1.00.

I had made up my mind. "I'll take it," I told the clerk. I thought in a very grown up manner. She put it in a little box and handed it to me.

"I wonder what I can get for Dad?"

She showed me the case of tie tacks, pens, and cigarette lighters. I saw a silver metal lighter that would be just right for Dad. She put it into another small box and laid it on top of the display case.

I walked over to the old fashioned cash register. It was made of gold metal and quite ornate. I proudly paid my bill with quarters.

Mission accomplished, we decided to stop at the Home Bakery and Café. We both agreed we needed to warm up.

Always thoughtful, Elma said, "We'll buy a few donuts and longjohns before we go home. Your folks and Mick would like a treat, too."

If you weren't hungry before you entered the Home Bakery you soon would be. The delicious smell of Mr. Carlson's baked goods hit your smeller as soon as you opened the door. We looked at the assortment of pastries in the front glass cases, then we walked back to the café area and chose a booth. Elma hung our wet coats on the hook.

I ordered a strawberry pop, and Elma ordered a root beer.

Elma told the waitress, "We'd like two bismarcks please."

I showed my purchases again to Elma. She seemed genuinely excited about the perfume, and I began to think.

"Your Mom is just going to love her gift, Honey," she added. "Anyone would love to get something so special, especially if they knew how long you had saved for it."

That was it. I had to do something.

"Elma, I think I forgot something at the drug store. Is it o.k. if I run and get it?"

"Go ahead, but be quick."

I walked as fast as I could the short distance to the drug store.

The clerk came and asked, "Did you forget something, Melanie?"

Lowering my voice, "No, but I've got to do this fast. Remember that perfume I got for Mom? Do you have another bottle?"

"Let's look. No, it looks like you bought the last one."

"Oh, no, that can't be!"

My disappointment was very evident.

"I'll look in the back room. Just wait a moment."

"I need to hurry." I hated to tell a fib to Elma, and I sure didn't want to make her worry about me taking so long.

The clerk rushed to the back room and came back shortly waving something in her hand. What a relief! I thanked her and gave her my money. I put the package in my pocket and hurried out of the drug store and into the Home Bakery. I quickly found my seat across from Elma.

"Did you find what you where looking for?" asked Elma.

I couldn't help but smile, "Yes, I did!"

Elma wasn't a great talker, and I was busy with my snack. We sat quietly drinking our pop and eating our jam-filled pastries.

The Home Cafe was full this afternoon. People were seated on the stools along the long counter and were crowded into the tables and booths.

Behind the counter large mirrors reflected the restaurant's customers. Also reflected were the ice cream freezers, malt machines, and the pop and coffee. The shelves were stacked with sundae, malt, and drink glasses. A long row of metal canisters held the various syrups and toppings for the ice cream creations.

On our way out, Elma and I stopped to buy a half dozen bismarcks and maple frosted longjohns. We trudged through the snow, already six or seven inches deep. This time I gave Elma my hand, and we started towards Erdman's grocery store.

We went straight to the candy aisle. Before us was a dazzling array of candies. We looked and pondered. You didn't want to rush these things. Elma reached for brightly colored ribbon candy, chocolate drops, and hard raspberry candies with a raspberry filling. I picked out the chocolate covered cherries.

"I think we need two boxes," she advised.

I didn't argue. Two boxes it was. Arms full of packages, we carefully walked the half block home. Opening the door, we were surrounded by warmth and Christmas music coming from the radio.

Mickey asked, "What did you get?"

Whispering in his ear, "I'll show you later."

"How would you like a treat now?" was Elma's happy news for my brother.

The candies rang against the bowl as Elma emptied the bag. I carefully placed the chocolate covered cherries onto a little dish. Mom put the donuts and longjohns on a plate.

Getting into the mood Mom asked, "Does anyone want a nice cup of hot tea?" She went to the living room, and invited Dad, "Melvin, come and join us."

With a mouth full of long john, Mickey asked, "I hope it snows all night, don't you, Mel?"

I agreed, but Mom didn't.

"You won't have time to play tomorrow, kids," she added, "We need to get to church in the morning, and don't forget your program is in the afternoon."

There was no way we could forget our Christmas program. Mom, Elma, and my Aunt Margaret were all Sunday school teachers and each had some role in the Christmas program. Mom's hope was that the snow would stop so we could make the five-mile trip to Dodge Center safe and sound.

"Well," Mom asked, "How was your shopping trip?"

I was so excited I almost slipped and spilled the beans, but I did tell her about the visit to Home Bakery.

"Mom, it's so pretty uptown. The snow is covering everything and all of the lights are on. You should go and see!"

Picking up the cups and plates she answered, "No, honey, it's getting too late. We have to start thinking about supper soon."

Later on that evening I took wrapping paper and tape up to my room. Mickey came up and I showed him what I had bought. I wrapped up both the gifts with bright red Christmas paper. I wrote out the tags and attached them to the packages. With a light step, I brought the four small packages downstairs and arranged them under the Christmas tree.

I gave Elma a goodnight kiss, "Thank you for taking me shopping today."

"You're welcome, sweetheart," she said, then she whispered, "I think your gift for your Mom is perfect."

I climbed the steep narrow stairs to my bedroom and crawled under the covers. As I lay there remembering what Elma had said, a smile spread over my face.

I called to Mickey across the hall, "Good night."

"Night, Mel," he answered back, and after a moment added, "I can't wait till tomorrow, can you?"

"No, I can't either." I gave a satisfied sigh, turned off my light, and happily went to sleep.

The Christmas program went well. We came home tired and happy.

The next day was Christmas eve. That night after coming home from my Aunt Margaret's house, Mickey and I put on our pajamas. We all gathered in the living room around the Christmas tree. Mickey and I passed out the gifts.

I watched as Dad and Mickey each opened a package. Then I opened a very large box from Mom and Dad. It contained a huge black and white panda bear. Then I noticed Mom and Elma each pick a present from the pile on their lap. Two small packages wrapped in shinny red paper. I shivered in anticipation. They started unwrapping them at the same time. Elma unwrapped the tissue around the bottle and quickly looked at Mom. Looking as if there had been a mistake, she watched as Mom pulled out the perfume.

"Thank you, Melanie," Mom unscrewed the cap. "Umm, Evening in Paris. It smells very nice."

Slowly a smile spread across Elma's face, as she also picked the perfume bottle out of its box.

Elma also opened her bottle to smell the fragrance. And then, with a twinkle in her eye, she looked into mine and said, "Thank you, Hon, what a perfect gift."

With my heart full of Christmas, I smiled "You're welcome."

The Ringing Of The Bells

"Mor! Mor!" Mother, Mother.

Someone was yelling. Inge, Helga, and Margit were busy doing breakfast dishes. Inge looked up quickly as her middle son, Hogin, burst through the heavy wooden door.

Shaking her head, "Slow down, for heaven's sake, Hogin. What is going on?"

Hogin stopped for a moment, "Don't you hear them, *Mor*, Mother? The bells are ringing. Listen, they just started."

Hogin raced into the next room. Inge wiped her hands on her long apron and walked to the door. She joined the two other women who quickly stepped out into the yard. Then they all stood in quiet expectation listening to a far off sound.

Helga closed her eyes and smiled, "*Ja*, yes, they have started. Do you hear them, girls?"

Inge and her sister-in-law Margit nodded in acknowledgement.

Inge thought to herself *at last*, and then answered her mother-in-law, "*Ja*, yes, I hear them, Helga. Don't they sound lovely?

"*Gledelig Jul*, Merry Christmas, Helga."

Helga turned and faced Inge, "*Gledelig Jul*, Merry Christmas, to you, too, Inge." And then Helga laughed out loud, "It has finally come."

Like the children, the women were eager for Christmas. Most of the preparations were complete. Now Christmas had officially arrived—the sounding of the bells announced the beginnings of the celebrations.

One of the oldest traditions in this northern Norwegian valley was the ringing in of Christmas. It would begin at the *Stave* church, the ancient wooden church located at the end of the valley in the village of Vaga.

Inge pictured Pastor Haugan pulling the bell rope. He loved making the old bells ring and told Inge once that this was one of his favorite jobs. Many others in the community loved this job also. Up and down the valley people were rushing to their own bells. As tradition dictated, when the first round of ringing sounded, each family brought out their bells to join in the ringing.

Hurrying back inside the house, the women quickly grabbed their shawls from the wooden hooks and tightly wrapped the heavy hand knitted wool garments around their heads and shoulders. Then they left the house and walked out into the snow-filled yard.

The pealing of the bells got louder by the minute. Gudbrandsdalen, a long valley with a broad river running the length, was a natural amphitheater.

Inge could feel a tingle of excitement at the pit of her stomach. She never lost the sense of wonder this day brought. Christmas offered a mix of comfort and exhilaration and brought back many good memories. Her mind drifted back to her parents' home. Often she had been the one ringing in Christmas.

As Inge listened intently to the bells, she heard another noise—it came from the children as they rushed out of the barn. Joseph, Inge's husband, his brother Sigurd, and Johannes, their *Far*, Father, also heard the bells. They had all been helping with chores, but once they heard the bells, all work stopped abruptly.

Although cold, Joseph took off his cap for a moment in respect for the Christ child. Sigurd and Johannes followed suit.

Inge was looking at her dark-haired husband when he asked, eyes searching the yard, "Where is Hogin?"

"In the house, getting the bells," smiled Inge. "He almost scared us to death; he came racing in like he had seen a ghost."

"If we had been by the door, he would have run us right over," laughed Joseph's mother, Helga.

Joseph smiled thinking of his son, then joined in the laughter, "*Ja*, yes, now I understand. He wasn't paying much attention to his chores this morning. I guess he had bells on his mind."

"Hogin was determined to ring in Christmas this year. He had his head cocked toward the door all morning," added Johannes.

Silence came over the Sannes family as they stood and listened. The sound of the bells came drifting down the valley. The slow, deep bong—bong—bong distinguished the church bells. Then the higher notes from the farm bells started to chime in. It was spellbinding. Hogin ran out of the house with his bells in tow. Hands over the clappers so they would remain silent until he joined his family. His *bestefar*, grandfather, was right—he had been listening for the bells all morning.

After Christmas last year, Hogin decided he was going to ring the bells this year. It was a great honor. Iver, his older brother, had won the right last year, and had talked and talked about it. Now Hogin would have something to talk about.

The deep sounds of the bells echoed off the valley walls. It became difficult to tell which direction the music came from. The family stood transfixed, listening to an almost unearthly composition.

"Go on, Hogin," encouraged Johannes. "You were the first. Let us hear those bells."

Excited, Hogin didn't need much coaxing. With solemn dignity, the young boy first lifted his right hand, then his left. The sound burst from the bells. The tempo was lost at first, but picked up until his bells became a part of the grand symphony. He seemed proud and very serious about his job. The sound came from everywhere, flowing up and down the valley. The whole community was participating.

A new set of bells was heard nearby. Someone from his *tante*, Aunt, Kari's farm next door was ringing their bells. Hogin didn't have time to wonder who. He rang on and on until he could barely lift his arms. His two brothers and cousins offered to help him, but he declined.

After what seemed like hours, the noise of the bells slowly started to abate. Hogin reluctantly quieted his own bells. Even when the last bell was silenced, the echoes still lingered in the air. No one seemed willing to move.

After a few minutes, Helga shivered, breaking the spell. "Brrr, let us go in. I'm getting too old for this cold. It reaches into my bones. Would anyone like some *sanbakkles* and milk?"

"What a good idea, Helga," Inge answered as she reached down and touched the blonde curly head of her youngest son, Ole. Looking at the children, she asked, "Could any of you children eat a cookie this morning?"

Not surprised at the overwhelming reception, Inge picked up her skirts and started toward the front door. The men walked toward the barn.

"We have about ten minutes of work left," Johannes said. "Helga, could you wait for us? We would like some of your good *sanbakkles* too."

Obviously pleased, Helga answered, "*Ja*, yes, we will get ready while you finish the chores. Boys, why don't you go back and help the men?" The older woman shivered again, "Come, Inge, Margit, let us go in."

Helga quickly walked inside the house. Taking off her shawl, she went to the table. Grabbing the coffee pot, she added more coffee to the breakfast grounds, then poured fresh water into the pot. Then she placed it back by the fire.

Inge went to the work table and unwrapped some of the Christmas cookies. Arranging them on a hand-carved wooden plate, she brought them to the big wooden table.

Within a short time the men came in, noisily stomping the snow off their boots.

The aroma of strong coffee greeted the men. "Um, smells good," Joseph commented to his mother as he walked into the room. He handed a pail of fresh milk to Inge, then hung his coat on a peg by the fire.

Helga stood by and watched Inge place a fresh pitcher of milk on the table. She motioned for the men to follow, "Come, sit. It's ready."

The men sat down at the table. Johannes looked at his grandson and smiled broadly, "Well, *takk*, thanks to Hogin, Christmas is officially here."

Johannes put his cold hands around the hot steaming cup of coffee. The warmth felt good on his work-worn hands. But before he took a sip, he said, "Let us ask God to bless this food on this special day."

The family bowed their heads, and Johannes led them in prayer.

"*Takk*, thank you, heavenly Father, for this food. We are blessed to have a warm home and delicious food to eat. We ask a special blessing for Hogin today. Accept his efforts to bring in this blessed holiday. Be with us throughout the day and evening. In your Son's name, Jesus."

Across the table, Joseph blew on his hot coffee. He took a sip. "Ahh, this is good, *Mor*, Mother, good, hot, and strong—just the way I like it." Then he looked at his son.

"Hogin, you did a fine job of ringing the bells today."

Everyone agreed. Not in the habit of hearing praise, Hogin looked down at the table and smiled. He was a proud and happy little boy. It had been a wonderful day already, and he thought to himself *this is just the start of Christmas*. His mouth watered at the thought of all the delicious food the women had been preparing for weeks.

Hogin knew the Christmas tree would be beautiful. He and his cousins helped select it and bring it down from the mountain. Then there would be singing and presents. It was all so exciting. Hogin thought he would explode.

The sound of the bells still seemed to ring in his ears. Thinking back to the bells, he wondered who had heard them first at *tante's*, Auntie's, house next door. He would soon find out, for they were all coming over tonight to start the celebration.

The Role Of A Lifetime

My heart was beating with excitement. The curtain was pulled, the blue light from the balcony clicked on, and out of the darkness came Joseph, baby Jesus, and me, Mary.

The crowd was hushed as they watched the little family in the stable. The journey for Mary and Joseph was over. This is how the play began—the young couple traveling to their ancestral home to pay taxes.

We had been rehearsing for weeks and weeks. Mostly at Sunday school, but songs and lines had been sent home to be practiced every day. As it got closer to Christmas, the rehearsals got longer and more serious.

What was I supposed to say? "You forgot your line. Enter shepherds. Angels do you know your place?" Our music director was trying to pull us all together in a cohesive group of actors and musicians. She had quite a job on her hands.

This year I was Mary. I went to a very small church in a small town. My people helped start the church and my mother and aunts were all Sunday school teachers.

It so happened that if you got to a certain age, and really wanted to play Mary, you usually got the part. This year I was fifteen, and I really wanted the part. I was chosen.

As I say, we had been practicing for weeks and slowly it was all coming together. We had dress rehearsal on Saturday. The pastor's office off the narthex was put into use as a waiting room for the actors to go onstage. It was very small, and we were crammed in like sardines.

We had hoped we had ironed out all of the kinks in the play. Almost everyone knew the songs and their lines. But there were still plenty of mistakes.

The wise men looked confident as they came onstage. But that changed when one of the Peterson twins tripped on his robe and bumped into his brother in front of him. Now with the domino effect in motion, he bumped into the next wise man. It could have been serious if two of the bigger angels hadn't come and grabbed them before they all tumbled down the steps.

I heard someone behind me comment, "They look more like the three stooges then the wise men."

I didn't think that was a nice thing to say, so I turned and gave him a nasty look, then quickly remembered who I was. Our director wasn't pleased with the comparison either and loudly tapped her baton on the music stand.

"Heads up, wise men, please get into your places, everyone else listen for your cues."

First down the aisle was the cherub choir. Smiley, wiggly, and giggly, they came to a stop at the alter. It was apparent they couldn't all stand still at the same time. When the director nodded and the piano began to play, they opened up and started to sing. The first verse loud and clear, but the subsequent ones faded off quickly. Their Sunday school teachers sang with them, helping with the words and actions.

"Oh, well," Mrs. Johnson said. "They will do better tomorrow."

Wishful thinking, I thought.

We ran through everything twice. That was it; tomorrow the play would go on.

We had been instructed to be at church on Sunday at three; the play was set for four. The first half of the play was Christmas music. After that we would be performing *The Journey*. Our costumes were in the pastor's office. Mine consisted of a blue cloth that would fasten under my chin. That was, it a long blue piece of material. Simple but effective.

Well this was it, the Sunday of the program. As it got closer to four, the younger children were assembled in the back of the church opposite the alter. They were waiting in three small rooms—a bathroom, a small annex, and a tiny kitchen.

In the corner, a large Christmas tree was brightly lit. The candles were lit in their stands and the ceiling lights were dimmed. The mood was set.

By four, the audience was seated and ready. The three, four, and five-year-olds came down the aisle, each with a bit of silver garland on their heads. We could hear the audience coo over these little ones. They were positioned by their teachers in front of the alter rail. The director raised her hand and the program began. "Away in the Manger" started out loud and clear. The motions were cute, though not in unison. One little boy leaned forward and shouted out the words. No one cared, just a muffled giggle here and there. They were cute and innocent and earnest in singing about the baby Jesus.

The cast of *The Journey* was crammed into the office. Angels, wise men, shepherds, the little family.

"Hey, watch it."

We all looked at Gabriel, his wings had gotten wedged between two of the shepherds.

"Can any of you guys move?"

As a body, we all moved a few feet to the right so the wing could be dislodged.

"There, if we can all just stand still," came from one of the wise men. Everyone nodded in agreement and tried very hard. But it proved too difficult for a couple of the smaller angels. They started to giggle.

But soon someone said, "Hush," in a loud whisper and quiet was restored.

The cherubs were singing "Jingle Bells," accompanying themselves enthusiastically with bells. The music ended, a shepherd peeked out, and said the cherubs were almost to the back of the church. The applause had stopped.

Now the six, seven, and eight-year-olds were coming down the aisle. They were dressed in their holiday best. The girls wore bright colored dresses—red, green, colorful plaids. A few were decked out in velvet and taffeta. The boys wore suits with ties or sweaters, shirts, and dress pants. "Deck The Halls" rang out loudly—the fa-la-las much louder than the verse. One little boy fa-la-la-ed when he should have been deck-the-halling. He stopped, stricken with embarrassment.

We all started to laugh, but sobered up quickly when each of us realized that could be one of us. Oh, please let us do this right.

Applause. The children smiled their thanks and burst into "Joy To The World."

The audience was getting into the production. Some were humming along with the music, but since it was a Scandinavian audience, they hummed stoically.

There was more applause as the children were led down the aisle back to the kitchen.

Back in the office it was getting harder to stand still. One of the shepherd's crooks nearly took out a light. A quick command burst out, " Lean them on the wall." By this time the room was quite warm and a musty odor was traced to the wise men's robes. How long had they been around?

The nine, ten, and eleven-year-olds began singing the English version of "O Christmas Tree" and then its counterpart, "O Tannenbaum," in German. The colored spotlight hit the tree in the corner, making it look all gold and shimmery; even the decorations the Sunday school classes had made looked great.

The singers started a bouncy "God Rest Ye Merry Gentlemen." The chorus, "O tidings of comfort and joy," resounded throughout our small church.

The audience stopped clapping and everything became quiet. One of us said, "Shush, Kathy Ann is next."

Out from behind the alter stepped Kathy Ann. She was sixteen and had one of the best voices in the church.

As she began singing "O, Holy Night," goose pimples climbed up my arms. I loved to sing too and wondered why Kathy Ann never seemed to get nervous. We admired her and we were all very quiet. When she was done, she stepped back to her "hiding spot" and the curtain closed.

Now it was our turn. From the other side of the curtain the director announced that the next part of the program was *The Journey*. While she was talking, we all scrambled, quietly, to our places. In the corner was the manger scene. Joseph and I were positioned in front of the manger.

A blue spotlight shown down on the sleeping shepherds, while a white one centered on Gabriel. He stood over the shepherds and announced with an authoritative voice, "Do not be afraid. I bring you good news of great joy that will be for all people. Today in the town of David a Savior has been born to you; He is Christ the Lord. This will be a sign to you: you will find a baby wrapped in cloths and lying in a manger."

Another angel came forward and said, "Glory to God in the highest, and on Earth, peace to men, on whom His favor rests."

So far so good; everyone was doing great!!

Then the lights flashed on a dozen angels, dressed in white robes, facing the shepherds with arms outstretched singing "Hark the Herald Angels Sing." The shepherds looked appropriately surprised.

After the angels sang "Angels From the Realms of Glory," ending with "Come and worship the new born king," the angels melted into the unlit background. One shepherd said to the others, "Let's go to Bethlehem and see this thing that has happened which the Lord has told us about." Off they went singing "O Little Town of Bethlehem."

I sat in the darkness quietly listening, touched by the music.

The shepherds started off for Bethlehem and into the darkness of the stage. Again the gold light illuminated the three wise men; they looked positively regal in their robes and turbans. The gifts they brought to the Christ child were impressive and rich.

With pomp and ceremony they arrived at the manger, singing "We Three Kings of Orient Are." They all sang the first stanza, then solos. Melchoir was first.

Melchoir: "Born a King on Bethlehem's plain, Gold I bring to crown him a King."

As I listened and watched, I was there. I began to feel as if I were at the stable and wished I had something to bring the baby. Casper came next.

Casper: "Frankincense to offer have I, Incense own a Deity."

Balthazar: "Myrrh is mine; its bitter perfume breathes a life of gathering doom."

They all sang the last verse, "Glorious now behold him arise, King and God and Sacrifice."

The audience was quiet; the wise men slipped into the darkness. The spotlight shone on one lone angel. Kathy Ann started to sing again looking directly at the manger. As she began, "What Child is This?" the blue spotlight lit up the manger scene.

"What child is this who laid to rest on Mary's lap is sleeping?" At my young age I was made keenly aware of this child lying in the manger. I looked lovingly at the baby. But that was easy.

Now all of the characters had arrived at the manger. They all knelt and worshipped the Christ child. I thought my heart would burst. What must Mary have thought?

Kathy ended the song with, "Joy, Joy for Christ is born, the babe, the son of Mary."

The spotlight shone on the manger scene: Joseph, Mary, and the baby Jesus, lit by the Bethlehem star. Slowly the light faded and the applause began, then came back up again. The music director stood and asked the audience to join us in "Silent Night."

The cast sang the first verse of that lovely old song, then the audience joined in. I looked out at Mom, Dad, Elma, Mick, my cousins, aunts and uncles, and others I knew almost as well. Everyone seemed to have been touched by this simple rendition of the Christmas story.

When the play was finished, all of us kids got our traditional bag of Christmas candy.

Mrs. Johnson said, "It was just lovely." Everyone joined in the praise. On the way home I was still wrapped in the afterglow of the music and the story.

That night I found it hard to go to sleep. The scenes kept playing in my head. But it was the finale that kept coming back to me. I could picture so vividly all the characters, from the humble shepherds to the majestic wise men, all bowing down to worship "the babe, the son of Mary."

"That babe, that son of Mary" is Jesus the Christ.

Jesus said:

"Come to me, all you who are weary and burdened, and I will give you rest. take my yoke upon you and learn from me, for I am gentle and humble in heart, and you will find rest for your souls.
For my yoke is easy and my burden is light."
Matt 11:28, 29 (NIV)

Come

Believe

Repent

Receive

Rest in His love

About the Author

Melanie Clifford worked in Christian counseling. A professional artist who has had her work commissioned by clients, Melanie also sells her paintings in art festivals and shows them in juried art shows. Melanie and her husband have three children and ten grandchildren and live in Minnesota.